RAMEN
FOR BEGINNERS

RAMEN
FOR BEGINNERS

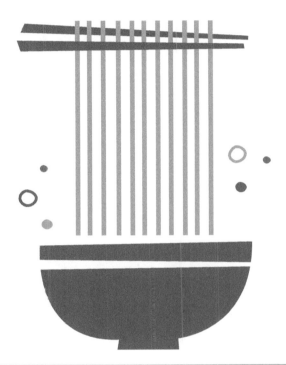

TRADITIONAL & MODERN
RECIPES MADE SIMPLE

ROBIN DONOVAN

PHOTOGRAPHY BY KATE SEARS

ROCKRIDGE
PRESS

For general information on our other products and services or to obtain technical support, please contact our Customer Care Department within the United States at (866) 744-2665, or outside the United States at (510) 253-0500.

Rockridge Press publishes its books in a variety of electronic and print formats. Some content that appears in print may not be available in electronic books, and vice versa.

TRADEMARKS: Rockridge Press and the Rockridge Press logo are trademarks or registered trademarks of Callisto Media Inc. and/or its affiliates, in the United States and other countries, and may not be used without written permission. All other trademarks are the property of their respective owners. Rockridge Press is not associated with any product or vendor mentioned in this book.

Interior and Cover Designer: Angela Navarra
Art Producer: Sara Feinstein
Editor: Kelly Koester
Production Editor: Rachel Taenzler

Photography © 2020 Kate Sears.
Food styling by Lori Powell.
Illustrations © 2020 Angela Navarra.

ISBN: Print 978-1-64611-281-4
eBook 978-1-64611-282-1
R0

For every ramen cook, whether you are just starting your ramen journey or are an accomplished master.

CONTENTS

INTRODUCTION

The story of ramen is fascinating because even though its history is relatively short within the grander scheme of Japanese cuisine, it has had a major cultural impact both in Japan and around the world.

A dish combining Chinese noodles and Japanese-style chicken broth was first introduced in Japan by Chinese travelers in the 1850s. The original dish was called Nanking soba after the capital city of China and was sold from food stalls and carts. Fifty-some years later, Rai-Rai Ken, a small shop employing Chinese chefs and selling bowls of shina soba (shina referring to China), opened in Tokyo. It was the first ramen-ya (ramen shop) in Japan. The dish gained popularity as a quick meal for blue-collar workers. By the 1950s, shina soba had become chüka soba (also meaning Chinese soba), as shina became a term of disparagement.

The noodles were, and still are, different from other wheat noodles like Italian pasta. They have a springy quality, achieved by adding an alkalinizing ingredient called kansui. In 1958, Momofuku Ando introduced packaged instant noodles that he called ramen (the word derives from the Japanese ra or la for "pulled" and men or mein for "noodles"). Over the next few decades, instant ramen became a household staple. Thanks to its low cost, ease of preparation, and appetizing combination of salt, fat, and carbs, it was embraced by busy parents, budget-tight students, and anyone looking for a quick meal on the cheap.

Meanwhile, ramen-ya—small, casual eateries serving inexpensive and hearty meals to working folks—began popping up across Japan. By the 1980s, ramen had become ubiquitous in Japanese culture, and ramen shops began striving to put their stamps of originality on the dish. Today, there are more than 6,000 ramen shops in the city of Tokyo alone. Every region of Japan has its own distinctive ramen style, and around the world you can find interpretations that incorporate local ingredients and cooking styles.

One of the most fascinating things about ramen is that it emerged from a cuisine that is dictated by centuries-old methods, but it is not bound by tradition. Ramen is able to adapt to its environment. Using local, seasonal ingredients is truer to the spirit of ramen than reproducing an established ideal. As a result, the possibilities for ramen creativity are literally limitless.

There are no real rules in ramen—it is anything-goes cuisine at its finest. Ramen chefs are free to experiment, borrow from other culinary traditions, and invent totally new parameters. Today you can wait for hours for a seat at a high-end, Michelin-starred ramen bar or pick up a 19-cent serving of packaged instant ramen at the corner store and cook it in your microwave, all under the umbrella of ramen.

Whether you make your own broth, noodles, seasoning sauces (tare), and toppings, or you buy all the components premade and simply assemble the dish to your liking, you can give it your own creative spin. When I make ramen at home, I usually use fresh or dried noodles that I buy from a neighborhood Japanese market. These can also be purchased in a large Asian supermarket, and the dried noodles are available in many supermarkets. You can also make your own noodles or use the noodles out of a package of instant ramen—you'll want to discard the flavoring packets that come with them.

I also like to keep homemade broth in my freezer because it is easy, inexpensive, and fun to make. But I have no qualms about using a can of broth from the grocery store. The same goes for toppings. Sometimes I buy frozen or ready-made toppings from the supermarket or Japanese grocery. Other times, I make my toppings from scratch or use very simple toppings that need only a bit of prep. This book provides recipes for making toppings from scratch, but for simplicity, I call out options for easily substituting store-bought versions as well.

This book is an easy guide to making ramen for home cooks who don't have the time, skill, or inclination to master fussy recipes or make every element from scratch. I encourage you to experiment with making your own broth, noodles, and toppings if that interests you. But know that the recipes in this book will still be delicious using store-bought ingredients.

While the recipes here are super simplified compared to those in other ramen cookbooks, the flavors and textures remain true to the spirit of "authentic ramen." Remember, making ramen is a creative endeavor. Don't get caught up in following the rules. Instead, let your imagination run wild. The results will be perfectly slurpable.

CHAPTER ONE

ASSEMBLING YOUR RAMEN-READY KITCHEN

Ramen has spawned cult-like devotion to particular chefs, restaurants, and styles, but at its core it is simply a bowl of noodles in a seasoned broth. Sure, a bowl of ramen can be an intricate and masterful work of art, but one of the great beauties of the dish is that it can be made from simple ingredients using basic kitchen tools. It can be elaborate, or it can simply be a tasty noodle soup.

STOCKING YOUR KITCHEN

Ramen is simple food, consisting of broth, seasonings, noodles, and toppings, and it doesn't require elaborate kitchen equipment or loads of special ingredients to make. In this chapter you'll find detailed information that will tell you everything you need to know to stock your ramen kitchen—from the pots you need to make and heat broth, to the ingredients you can't make ramen without, to the bowls you'll serve the soup in. Rest assured, you likely have many of the items you need in your kitchen already.

THE POTS

To make a great soup, you'll want to start with a nice big pot. In the case of ramen, you'll need two nice big pots—one for the broth and one for the noodles—as well as a few other pots and pans for making the toppings.

FOR THE TOPPINGS: You'll need basic pots and pans like those that you probably have in your kitchen. A medium skillet and small and large saucepans will work for all the toppings in this book.

FOR THE BROTH: If you are making broth from scratch, you'll need a stockpot large enough to fit bones and water, ideally a 6-quart or larger one. For heating store-bought broth, a smaller pot, 3 to 4 quarts, is fine.

FOR THE NOODLES: For cooking the noodles, a 4- to 6-quart saucepan or stockpot is perfect.

THE SOUP BOWLS

A good bowl is integral to the ramen-eating experience. If the bowl is too deep, the noodles will sink to the bottom and be difficult to pick up. A bowl that is too narrow won't allow space to arrange your toppings creatively on top. A too-shallow or too-wide bowl will let the soup cool off too quickly.

The perfect ramen bowl is large enough to comfortably fit a good-size portion of noodles and broth with space to arrange several toppings on top. Ideally, when fully constructed, a ramen bowl with noodles, broth, and toppings will be 80 percent full, to prevent spillage.

Here is a guide to bowl sizes:

→ A small ramen bowl is about 7½ inches across and holds approximately 34 ounces (a little more than 4 cups).

→ A medium ramen bowl is 8 inches across and holds about 45 ounces (a little over 5½ cups).

→ A large ramen bowl is 9 inches across and holds 58 ounces (more than 7 cups).

For serving ramen at home, small and medium ramen bowls are ideal.

THE UTENSILS

Ramen requires at least two utensils to eat. The first is a spoon for the broth. The typical ramen spoon is a wide, flat Chinese-style spoon that is perfect for scooping up ramen broth.

Chopsticks are typically used to eat the noodles and toppings in a bowl of ramen and are conducive to slurping the noodles straight from the bowl, which is considered good manners in Japanese culture. Some say slurping helps cool the noodles down as you eat them, and that it also accentuates the flavors.

Japanese chopsticks are shorter and pointier than Chinese chopsticks and can be made of bamboo or wood. They are often coated with lacquer. If you don't have chopsticks or aren't comfortable using them, go ahead and use a fork. No matter what utensil you use to eat your ramen noodles, they're sure to be delicious!

THE PANTRY MUST-HAVES

Once you start making your own ramen at home, you'll discover how easy and satisfying it is, and hopefully you'll want to make it regularly. To that end, keep your pantry stocked with a few essentials, and you'll always be prepared to cook up a piping-hot bowl. In addition to broth, noodles, and an assortment of meat, fish, and vegetables for toppings, here is a list of basic seasonings and pantry items you will find yourself reaching for as you explore the world of homemade ramen. Many of these items can be found in chain supermarkets, but for some you might have to go to an Asian market or order online.

→ Cooking oil. Use any neutral-flavored, high-smoke-point oil when this is called for in a recipe. These include vegetable oil, corn oil, canola oil, peanut oil, and safflower oil.

→ Flavored oils (sesame, chili)

→ Fresh herbs/aromatics (ginger, garlic, cilantro, scallions, jalapeño peppers, limes, lemons)

→ Sesame seeds

→ Sauces (soy sauce, sriracha, chili paste/sambal oelek, hoisin sauce, oyster sauce)

→ Japanese or Chinese sesame paste. You can find this in some supermarkets, in Asian markets, or online. This is a toasted sesame paste that has a rich, nutty flavor. If you can't find it, don't be tempted to substitute tahini, which is a more lightly toasted sesame paste and won't provide the right flavor. Instead, substitute a creamy, no-sugar-added peanut butter.

→ Doubanjiang (Chinese fermented bean paste) and spicy doubanjiang. You can find these in Asian markets or online.

→ Miso paste. Miso pastes vary in flavor from mild to very salty and intense. Generally speaking, the lighter the color of the miso, the milder it is. White miso, or shiro miso, is mild. Red miso, or aka miso, is more intense. Awase miso is a combination of white and red miso pastes, with a flavor that falls in between the two. I keep both white and red miso in my refrigerator and often use a mixture of the two. If you want to buy only one, start with white/shiro miso. Look for miso paste in the refrigerator section of Asian markets and some large supermarkets. You can also buy miso paste online.

CHAPTER TWO

THE BUILDING BLOCKS OF RAMEN: BROTH, NOODLES, AND SEASONINGS

When you get down to basics, ramen is just a simple yet flavorful noodle soup—a bowl of savory broth filled with chewy noodles and enhanced with seasonings and toppings. To build a delicious bowl of ramen, you start with your broth or base, then add your seasoning sauce ("tare" in Japanese), noodles, and toppings.

WHAT BROTH BRINGS TO YOUR BOWL

Unlike many other soups, the flavor in ramen comes more from seasoning mixtures (tare) than from the broth itself. The broth used in ramen is usually very simple and made from only two or three ingredients such as water and pork, or chicken, bones. "Double broth" ramens combine two different broths, such as a pork (tonkostu) broth combined with a fish-and-seaweed-broth (awase dashi).

Ramen broths are distinguished by the basic ingredients (pork, chicken, mushrooms) used to make them: chicken broth (tori chintan), pork broth (tonkostu), or mushroom broth (shiitake dashi) are a few of the most common ramen broths.

Ramen masters make their own broth by boiling bones (pork, chicken, duck, or beef), seaweed, dried mushrooms, or dried fish. If you have the time and inclination to make broth from scratch, by all means, go for it. It's not hard, just a bit time-consuming.

If you want to skip the process of making broth from scratch, you can absolutely substitute store-bought broth or make quick broths with seasonings and water. Here are the types of broth that will be used in the recipes in this book.

CHICKEN BROTH

Chicken broth makes a great and versatile base for ramen. It is rich and flavorful without overpowering the other seasonings in the bowl. If you don't make it yourself, you can buy chicken broth in cans, cartons, or jars, or you can even use bouillon cubes, powder, or concentrate in its place.

BASIC CHICKEN BROTH (TORI CHINTAN)

5-INGREDIENT, DAIRY-FREE, GLUTEN-FREE, MAKE IT AHEAD, NUT-FREE
PREP TIME: 15 MINUTES / **COOK TIME:** 6 HOURS
MAKES ABOUT 8 CUPS

3 pounds chicken bones	1 pound chicken feet, blanched, drained, and rinsed	1 pound chicken wings 10 to 12 cups water

1. In a large stockpot put the chicken bones, feet, and wings, and add the water. Set the pot over low heat, bring to a simmer, and skim off any foam that rises to the top. Cover the pot and simmer for 6 hours.

2. Place a strainer or colander over a large bowl, pour the broth into it, and discard the solids.

3. Let the broth cool to room temperature and then refrigerate it for at least 4 hours.

4. Skim the fat off the top of the broth (if you'd like, you can save it and use it to season your ramen or as a cooking fat).

STORAGE TIP: Store the broth in an airtight container in the refrigerator for up to 1 week or in the freezer for up to 3 months.

COOKING TIP: For the bone broth recipes, blanching of some or all of the bones is required before making the broth. To blanch the bones and chicken feet in this recipe, or the bones in any other recipe, put them in a stockpot covered by a couple of inches of water and bring to a boil. Boil for about 15 minutes and drain. Rinse well before proceeding with the recipe.

PORK BROTH

Pork broth is featured at many popular ramen restaurants, but it can be harder to find in the supermarket than chicken or beef broth. Look for pork broth base, paste, or bouillon in some supermarkets, Asian markets, or online. Tonkotsu is a style of ramen broth made by boiling pork bones for many hours and is extremely rich and full of collagen, which gives it a thick, viscous consistency.

BASIC PORK BROTH (TONKOTSU)

5-INGREDIENT, DAIRY-FREE, GLUTEN-FREE, MAKE IT AHEAD, NUT-FREE
PREP TIME: 15 MINUTES / **COOK TIME:** 10 HOURS
MAKES ABOUT 8 CUPS

4 to 5 pounds pork
   bones, cut into
   2- to 3-inch pieces,
   blanched, drained,
   and rinsed

1 onion, peeled
   and halved
12 to 16 cups water

1. In a large stockpot, combine the bones, onion, and water. Bring to a boil over high heat. Reduce the heat to medium and skim off the brown foam that rises to the top, then reduce the heat to low and simmer for 8 hours. To keep the bones covered, add water if needed.

2. Raise the heat to high and bring to a rolling boil. Cook at a hard boil, occasionally stirring vigorously with a wooden spoon, for another 1 to 2 hours.

3. Place a strainer or colander over a large bowl, pour the broth into it, and discard the solids.

4. Let the broth cool to room temperature and then refrigerate it for at least 4 hours.

5. Skim the fat off the top of the broth (if you'd like, you can save it and use it to season your ramen or as a cooking fat).

STORAGE TIP: Store the broth in an airtight container in the refrigerator for up to 1 week or in the freezer for up to 3 months.

BEEF BROTH

Beef broth is not common in traditional ramen, but it makes a nice base for a meaty bowl of ramen nonetheless. Like chicken broth, beef broth is widely available in cans, cartons, and jars, as well as in bouillon cubes, powder, or paste, or you can make it yourself with this recipe.

BASIC BEEF BROTH

5-INGREDIENT, DAIRY-FREE, GLUTEN-FREE, MAKE IT AHEAD, NUT-FREE
PREP TIME: 15 MINUTES / **COOK TIME:** 10 HOURS
MAKES 8 CUPS

4 to 5 pounds beef
  bones, cut into
  2- to 3-inch pieces,
  blanched, drained,
  and rinsed

1 onion, peeled
  and halved
12 to 16 cups water

1. In a large stockpot, combine the beef bones, onion, and water. Bring to a boil over high heat. Reduce the heat to medium and skim off the brown foam that rises to the top, then cook at c hearty simmer for 8 hours. To keep the bones covered, add water if needed.

2. Raise the heat to high and bring to a rolling boil. Cook at a hard boil, occasionally stirring vigorously with a wooden spoon, for another 1 to 2 hours.

3. Place a strainer or colander over a large bowl, pour the broth into it, and discard the solids.

4. Let the broth cool to room temperature and then refrigerate it for at least 4 hours.

5. Skim the fat off the top of the broth (if you'd like, you can save it and use it to season your ramen or as a cooking fat).

STORAGE TIP: Store the broth in the refrigerator for up to 1 week or in the freezer for up to 3 months.

FISH BROTH

Fish broth is often used for lighter ramens featuring fish or seafood toppings. Fish broth is easy to make at home by combining dried bonito flakes with boiling water. You can buy bonito flakes in many supermarkets (in the international foods aisle), in Asian markets, or online.

BASIC FISH BROTH (KATSUO DASHI)

5-INGREDIENT, 30 MINUTES OR LESS, DAIRY-FREE, GLUTEN-FREE, MAKE IT AHEAD, NUT-FREE

PREP TIME: 5 MINUTES, PLUS 15 MINUTES TO LET REST / **COOK TIME:** 5 MINUTES

MAKES 8 CUPS

---

8 cups water

4 cups dried bonito flakes

1. In a stockpot, bring the water to a boil over high heat.

2. Add the bonito flakes and simmer for 30 seconds, then remove the pot from the heat.

3. Let the mixture stand at room temperature for about 15 minutes.

4. Pour the broth through a fine-mesh sieve set over a bowl, and discard the bonito flakes.

STORAGE TIP: Store the broth in an airtight container in the refrigerator for up to 1 week or in the freezer for up to 3 months.

VEGAN BROTH

Vegan broth is usually made with dried kelp (kombu), dried shiitake mushrooms, or a combination of the two. You can find these ingredients in Asian markets and in the international foods aisle of many supermarkets.

BASIC VEGAN BROTH (KOMBU DASHI)

5-INGREDIENT, 30 MINUTES OR LESS, DAIRY-FREE, GLUTEN-FREE, MAKE IT AHEAD, NUT-FREE, VEGAN

PREP TIME: 5 MINUTES / **COOK TIME:** 10 MINUTES

MAKES 8 CUPS

---

2 (4-inch) squares dried sea kelp (kombu)

8 cups water

1. Cut a few slits into each piece of kombu.

2. In a stockpot, combine the water and kombu and bring to a near boil over medium-high heat for about 10 minutes.

3. Remove the kombu from the pot and remove the pot from the heat.

4. Let the broth cool to room temperature and then refrigerate it.

STORAGE TIP: Store the broth in an airtight container in the refrigerator for up to 1 week or in the freezer for up to 3 months.

MUSHROOM BROTH (SHIITAKE DASHI)

5-INGREDIENT, DAIRY-FREE, GLUTEN-FREE, MAKE IT AHEAD, NUT-FREE, VEGAN
PREP TIME: 5 MINUTES / **COOK TIME:** 5 MINUTES, PLUS 30 MINUTES TO LET REST
MAKES 8 CUPS

8 cups water

3 ounces dried shiitake mushrooms, stemmed and cut into strips

1. In a stockpot, combine the water and dried mushrooms, and over medium-high heat bring to a simmer.

2. Remove the pot from the heat and let stand for about 30 minutes.

3. Strain the mushrooms out of the broth. (Save the mushrooms and add them to your soup, if desired.)

STORAGE TIP: Store in an airtight container in the refrigerator for up to 1 week or in the freezer for up to 3 months.

RAMEN RESCUED: HOW TO FIX TOO-SALTY BROTH

What's a ramen cook to do when their ramen broth is too salty? Maybe you slipped and drizzled in too much tare, soy sauce, or salt? Don't fret! You have options:

1. Dilute the broth either by adding water or by making a second batch of broth with no added salt. Mix this new batch with the too-salty batch and all is forgiven. Freeze whatever you don't need right away. You can never have too much broth in your freezer.

2. Add acid. Add lemon, lime, yuzu, other juice, vinegar, sake, or other wine. The acid will balance the salt, making the broth taste less salty.

3. Leave out the salt or greatly reduce the quantity when cooking the noodles and toppings. Starchy ingredients like noodles will especially help absorb salt from the broth and balance out the flavors in the bowl of soup.

KNOW YOUR NOODLES

No ramen is complete without noodles. Ramen noodles are wheat noodles that have been treated with an alkalinizing agent, called kansui, to give them their distinctive springy texture. They come in several forms: fresh, dried, instant, or gluten-free.

FRESH RAMEN NOODLES are always my first choice because they have minimal ingredients, cook up to the ideal chewy-tender texture, and absorb the other flavors in the soup especially well. If you have a Japanese market in your area, you can likely get great-quality fresh or fresh-frozen noodles there. If not, you might try asking your favorite ramen restaurant if they would sell you a bag of their noodles. Keep them in the refrigerator, or pop them in the freezer, where they'll last for months. You can cook them straight out of the refrigerator or freezer—about 3 minutes in boiling water (30 to 60 seconds more for frozen noodles).

DRIED RAMEN NOODLES take a bit longer to cook, but they are a great option if fresh noodles aren't available. Look for them in the Asian foods aisle in the supermarket or in any Asian market in the noodles aisle.

INSTANT RAMEN NOODLES are flash-fried before packaging, which is what makes them so quick. I admit it: I always have a few packs of instant ramen in my pantry simply because they are so quick to make. I also love that my 11-year-old son can make himself a bowl on his own.

GLUTEN-FREE NOODLES. Ramen noodles are wheat noodles by definition, but if you are on a gluten-free diet (or cooking for someone who is), you can substitute Asian rice noodles such as Vietnamese rice vermicelli or Thai rice stick noodles. They are made using rice flour, so they are naturally gluten-free. The taste and texture won't be the same as real ramen noodles, but these noodles are delicious and work well in soup. You can buy rice noodles in most supermarkets in the international foods aisle, or in any Asian grocery.

RAMEN RESCUED:
HOW TO SAVE OVERCOOKED NOODLES

Every ramen cook has been there: You take your eyes off the pot for a second too long, and suddenly you have overcooked noodles. Rest assured, there are a few solutions to this soggy conundrum.

1. Stir-fry the noodles in a bit of oil in a hot pan to crisp them up and then add them to a bowl of ramen or eat them on their own.
2. Toss the hot noodles with cheese, which will disguise their limpness. Plus, what dish can't be improved with a bunch of melty cheese?
3. Toss the noodles in a flavorful dressing or sauce—sesame sauce, peanut sauce, or a miso-ginger dressing, for instance—and then chill them to firm up their texture.

SEASONING YOUR RAMEN

In ramen shops, the flavors in a bowl of ramen are created by layering broth and a tare (seasoning sauce) before adding noodles, toppings, and other seasonings. There are a few common types of tare, which are distinguished by their main seasoning ingredient. Shio tare gets most of its flavor from salt. Shoyu tare derives its flavor from soy sauce. Miso tare starts with a base of miso (fermented soybean) paste. Other ingredients round out the tares, like rice wine, vinegar, sugar, chile paste, and seasame oil. These mixtures are what give each bowl of ramen its distinct flavor. By combining broths and tares in different combinations, you can achieve a wide range of ramen flavor experiences.

You can mix up these tares in large batches and keep them in your refrigerator, making it easy to whip up a flavorful bowl anytime. These are the tares used in the recipes in this book.

SHIO TARE

Shio ("salt" in Japanese) tare is primarily flavored by salt or salty ingredients like dried anchovies. But the flavor of a good shio tare goes beyond just saltiness. Other ingredients like seaweed, mushrooms, sugar, mirin (sweet rice wine), sake, or dried fish flakes (bonito) add layers of complex flavor and umami. This version is vegan, but for even more depth of flavor, you can add dried fish flakes, dried anchovies (niboshi), or fish sauce.

BASIC SHIO TARE

5-INGREDIENT, DAIRY-FREE, GLUTEN-FREE, MAKE IT AHEAD, NUT-FREE, ONE-POT, VEGAN

PREP TIME: 5 MINUTES / **COOK TIME:** 1 HOUR

MAKES ABOUT 2 CUPS

1 cup water	¼ cup mirin	½ cup salt
1 cup sake	1 (4-inch) piece kombu	

1. In a medium saucepan, bring the water to a boil. Add the sake, mirin, and kombu. Reduce heat to low, cover, and simmer gently for 1 hour.

2. Remove the pot from the heat, discard the kombu, stir in the salt until it dissolves, and let the mixture cool to room temperature.

3. For each bowl of ramen, use about 2 tablespoons of the mixture.

STORAGE TIP: Store shio tare in an airtight container in the refrigerator for up to 3 weeks or in the freezer for up to 3 months.

SHOYU TARE

Shoyu tare is the most traditional ramen seasoning base. In its most basic form, it is a mixture of soy sauce and rice wine. The flavor can be amped up by adding other ingredients like seaweed, dried fish, chile paste, sugar, garlic, and/or ginger. In the spirit of simplicity and ease, this shoyu tare only adds sugar to the mixture to balance out the saltiness.

BASIC SHOYU TARE

5-INGREDIENT, 30 MINUTES OR LESS, DAIRY-FREE, MAKE IT AHEAD, NUT-FREE, ONE-POT, VEGAN

PREP TIME: 5 MINUTES / **COOK TIME:** 5 MINUTES

MAKES ABOUT 2 CUPS

---

1 cup soy sauce
½ cup sake

½ cup mirin
1 tablespoon sugar

1. In a medium saucepan, combine the soy sauce, sake, mirin, and sugar, and bring the mixture to a boil. Quickly reduce the heat to low and simmer, stirring, until the sugar is dissolved, about 3 minutes. Remove the pan from the heat and let the mixture cool to room temperature.

2. For each bowl of ramen, use about 2 tablespoons of the mixture.

STORAGE TIP: Store shoyu tare in an airtight container in the refrigerator for up to 3 weeks or in the freezer for up to 3 months.

MISO TARE

Miso tare starts with a base of miso paste. It is rich, salty, and full of umami. Like the other tares, miso tare often also includes ingredients like sake, mirin, soy sauce, and aromatics such as ginger or garlic. Some miso tares are spicy, getting a kick from dried or fresh chiles, chili paste, or chili oil.

BASIC MISO TARE

5-INGREDIENT, 30 MINUTES OR LESS, DAIRY-FREE, GLUTEN-FREE, MAKE IT AHEAD, NUT-FREE OPTION, ONE-POT, VEGAN

PREP TIME: 5 MINUTES

MAKES ABOUT 1½ CUPS

½ cup miso paste (use white/shiro miso, awase miso, or half-and-half white/shiro miso and red/aka miso)

¼ cup salt

¼ cup water

3 tablespoons Japanese sesame paste or creamy no-sugar-added peanut butter

2 tablespoons sesame oil

1 tablespoon rice vinegar

1. In a medium bowl, stir the miso paste, salt, water, sesame paste, sesame oil, and rice vinegar together.

2. For each bowl of ramen, use about 2 tablespoons of the mixture.

STORAGE TIP: Store miso tare in an airtight container in the refrigerator for up to 3 weeks or in the freezer for up to 3 months.

VARIATION TIP: To make Spicy Miso Tare, add ¼ cup of chili paste (such as sambal oelek) or gochujang (Korean fermented chili paste) to the recipe.

*From clockwise: Sesame-Chili Oil, **page 30**; Seasoned Bamboo Shoots, **page 22**; Soy Sauce Eggs, **page 28**; Sunomono, **page 26***

CHAPTER THREE

TOPPINGS

The possible combinations for topping a bowl of ramen are literally endless, but there are a few common toppings that are delicious, easy to prepare, and great for making ahead and having on hand. From simple marinated vegetables to complexly flavored infused oils, the toppings in this chapter can be added to just about any bowl of ramen to give it your own personal spin.

A good bowl of ramen should boast a juxtaposition of textures and flavors—such as soft, crunchy, cooling, spicy, savory, and sweet.

This chapter includes some of the most traditional, simple, and common toppings like soft-boiled eggs and preserved bamboo shoots (menma). You'll find numerous topping ideas in the later chapters, too, where the recipes include things like fried chicken and roasted vegetables to crown their bowls.

The vegetables can also double as appetizers or side dishes. The eggs, both soft-boiled and soy-sauce-marinated, make great snacks or lunchbox additions. The oils and the seasoning mixture can be put on the table for diners to add at their own discretion, and they can be used to dress up more than just ramen, too.

SEASONED BAMBOO SHOOTS

30 MINUTES OR LESS, DAIRY-FREE, MAKE IT AHEAD, NUT-FREE, ONE-POT, VEGAN
PREP TIME: 5 MINUTES / **COOK TIME:** 20 MINUTES
MAKES ABOUT 2 CUPS

Seasoned bamboo shoots (menma) are a popular ramen topping in Japan. Bamboo shoots are the delicate shoots of young bamboo plants. Braised in soy sauce and rice wine, they add nice sweet-savory flavor and a bit of crunch. Fresh bamboo shoots, which you can find in Asian markets, provide the best flavor and texture.

8 ounces fresh bamboo shoots, cut into strips

1 cup Basic Vegan Broth (page 13) **or water**

1½ teaspoons sesame oil

1½ teaspoons soy sauce

1½ teaspoons sake or rice wine

1½ teaspoons sugar

½ teaspoon kosher salt

1. In a medium saucepan, combine the bamboo shoots, broth, sesame oil, soy sauce, sake, sugar, and salt, and bring to a boil over high heat.

2. Reduce the heat to medium and simmer the mixture for about 20 minutes, until the liquid has mostly evaporated.

SUBSTITUTION TIP: If you can't find fresh bamboo shoots, you can substitute canned. They won't be quite the same as the fresh version, but simmering them with the seasonings will get rid of any canned flavor.

MARINATED BEAN SPROUTS

30 MINUTES OR LESS, DAIRY-FREE, MAKE IT AHEAD, NUT-FREE, VEGAN
PREP TIME: 10 MINUTES / **COOK TIME:** 5 MINUTES, PLUS 15 MINUTES TO LET REST
MAKES ABOUT 2 CUPS

This simple sesame–soy sauce dressing and marinade transforms crunchy bean sprouts into the perfect topping for a bowl of ramen. It is simple to make and adds both flavor and texture to the bowl. If you've made the Shichimi Togarashi (page 31) or have a bottle of the store-bought version, sprinkle a bit on top for even more flavor.

1 cup water
12 ounces bean sprouts
2 tablespoons sesame oil
1½ teaspoons soy sauce
½ teaspoon kosher salt

¼ teaspoon freshly
   ground black pepper
¼ teaspoon red
   pepper flakes

2 scallions, both white
   and green parts,
   thinly sliced
1 tablespoon toasted
   sesame seeds

1. In a medium saucepan, bring the water to a boil. Add the bean sprouts and cook for about 30 seconds. Drain in a colander and rinse well with cold water. Press down on the sprouts to remove excess water.

2. In a medium bowl, whisk together the sesame oil, soy sauce, salt, pepper, and red pepper flakes. Stir in the scallions, sesame seeds, and bean sprouts. Let the sprouts stand for at least 15 minutes, then serve.

STORAGE TIP: Store leftover bean sprouts in an airtight container in the refrigerator for up to 5 days.

ROASTED TOMATOES

5-INGREDIENT, DAIRY-FREE, GLUTEN-FREE, MAKE IT AHEAD, NUT-FREE, VEGAN
PREP TIME: 10 MINUTES / **COOK TIME:** 30 MINUTES
MAKES 24 TOMATO HALVES

Roasted tomatoes are one of my favorite unconventional ramen toppings. The idea was introduced by an American ramen master, Ivan Orkin. Even though tomatoes aren't native to Japanese cuisine, they bring a deep umami that fits right in with a bowl of savory ramen.

12 plum tomatoes, halved

3 tablespoons
   extra-virgin olive oil

1 teaspoon kosher salt

½ teaspoon freshly
   ground black pepper

1. Preheat the oven to 450°F.

2. In a bowl, toss the tomatoes and olive oil together to coat the tomatoes well. Arrange the tomatoes on a large rimmed baking sheet, cut-side up. Sprinkle the tomatoes with the salt and pepper.

3. Roast the tomatoes for about 30 minutes, until they are very tender and are beginning to brown on the edges.

STORAGE TIP: This is best when made with height-of-the-season tomatoes. I like to make a giant batch of them in late summer when supersweet plum tomatoes are abundant and usually on sale. Store the roasted tomatoes in the refrigerator for up to 1 week or in the freezer for up to 6 months.

CRISPY KALE

5-INGREDIENT, 30 MINUTES OR LESS, DAIRY-FREE, GLUTEN-FREE, MAKE IT AHEAD, NUT-FREE, VEGAN

PREP TIME: 5 MINUTES / **COOK TIME:** 15 MINUTES

MAKES ABOUT 4 CUPS

Crispy kale leaves are a fun, healthy way to add texture to a bowl of ramen. The result is similar to using toasted nori (seaweed) sheets. Be sure to add the kale to the ramen just before serving so that it stays crisp. Or put it in a bowl on the table and let diners add it in small amounts while they eat.

---

12 leaves kale, tough center stems removed, torn into large pieces	**1 tablespoon extra-virgin olive oil** **1 teaspoon sesame oil**	**Kosher salt** **Freshly ground black pepper**

1. Preheat the oven to 425°F.

2. On a large baking sheet, toss the kale with the olive oil and sesame oil. Arrange the kale in a single layer. Season it with salt and pepper.

3. Roast for about 15 minutes, until crisp.

VARIATION TIP: You can spice up your kale however you like by sprinkling on dried spices before roasting. Try a pinch or two of chili powder, curry powder, or ground cumin.

SUNOMONO (QUICK-PICKLED CUCUMBER SALAD)

5-INGREDIENT, 30 MINUTES OR LESS, DAIRY-FREE, MAKE IT AHEAD, NUT-FREE, VEGAN

PREP TIME: 10 MINUTES, PLUS 10 MINUTES TO MARINATE

SERVES 4

Pickles (tsukemono) are often served alongside Japanese meals. This quick pickle of thinly sliced cucumbers is made by salting cucumber slices to draw out excess moisture and help them absorb flavor, and then tossing them in a mixture of rice vinegar, sugar, and soy sauce.

2 Japanese cucumbers, thinly sliced

¼ teaspoon kosher salt

¼ cup unseasoned rice vinegar

1 tablespoon granulated sugar

¼ teaspoon soy sauce

1 teaspoon black or white sesame seeds

1. In a medium bowl, toss the cucumbers with the salt. Let them stand for about 5 minutes to draw some of the water out of the cucumbers.

2. Meanwhile, in a jar or small bowl, shake or whisk together the vinegar, sugar, and soy sauce. Whisk or shake until the sugar is fully dissolved.

3. Pour the vinegar mixture over the cucumbers and toss to combine. Let the salad stand for about 10 minutes, or chill until ready to serve.

4. Just before serving, garnish with the sesame seeds.

SUBSTITUTION TIP: If you don't have Japanese cucumbers, substitute 4 Persian cucumbers. Or use 1 English cucumber, halved lengthwise, with the seeds scooped out.

SOFT-BOILED EGGS

5-INGREDIENT, 30 MINUTES OR LESS, DAIRY-FREE, GLUTEN-FREE, MAKE IT AHEAD, NUT-FREE, VEGETARIAN

PREP TIME: 10 MINUTES / **COOK TIME:** 5 MINUTES

MAKES 6 EGGS

Soft-boiled eggs are among the most common toppings for ramen. If you are dining at a trendy ramen shop, you're more than likely to find a perfectly cooked soft-boiled egg adorning your bowl, and you may want to do the same to dress up your ramen bowl at home.

**6 large eggs, at
   room temperature**

1. Fill a medium saucepan with water and bring it to a boil over high heat. Reduce the heat to medium so that the water is simmering just below boiling. Using a slotted spoon, gently lower the eggs into the water. Simmer for 6 minutes.

2. While the eggs are simmering, put several ice cubes into a large bowl and add cold water to cover them.

3. When the eggs are finished cooking, pour off the hot water and run cold water over them for a few minutes to cool them down. Transfer the eggs to the ice bath and let them sit for about 5 minutes, until they are completely cooled. Drain.

4. To serve, carefully peel the eggs and slice them in half lengthwise.

STORAGE TIP: Soft-boiled eggs will keep, unpeeled, in the refrigerator for up to 5 days. You can use these eggs to make Soy Sauce Eggs (page 28).

SOY SAUCE EGGS

DAIRY-FREE, MAKE IT AHEAD, NUT-FREE, VEGETARIAN
PREP TIME: 5 MINUTES / **COOK TIME:** 5 MINUTES, PLUS 8 HOURS TO MARINATE
MAKES 6 EGGS

Soft-boiled eggs are a quintessential ramen topping superseded only by these, which are soft-boiled eggs that have been marinated in a mixture of soy sauce, rice wine, sugar, and ginger. After you've made a batch of soft-boiled eggs, it's a cinch to turn some or all of them into soy sauce eggs. They make a great ramen topping but are also perfect for snacking.

¾ cup reduced-sodium
   soy sauce
¾ cup water
½ cup sake

¼ cup mirin
1 tablespoon sugar
2 teaspoons chopped
   fresh ginger

6 Soft-Boiled Eggs
   (page 27), **peeled**

1. In a medium saucepan, combine the soy sauce, water, sake, mirin, sugar, and ginger, and bring the mixture to a boil over high heat. Reduce the heat to medium-low and simmer for about 3 minutes, stirring frequently, until the sugar dissolves completely.

2. Transfer the mixture to a jar or container large enough to hold both the marinade and the eggs, and let it cool for about 20 minutes to room temperature.

3. Add the peeled eggs to the soy sauce mixture, cover the jar, and refrigerate for about 8 hours (do not leave them for longer than 12 hours). Remove the eggs from the marinade, cut them in half lengthwise, and serve as a topping on ramen.

STORAGE TIP: Store soy sauce eggs in an airtight container in the refrigerator for up to 3 days.

SCALLION OIL

5-INGREDIENT, DAIRY-FREE, GLUTEN-FREE, MAKE IT AHEAD, NUT-FREE, VEGAN
PREP TIME: 5 MINUTES / **COOK TIME:** 45 MINUTES
MAKES ABOUT 1 CUP

Scallion oil is easy to make, and it adds real depth of flavor to a bowl of ramen. Let it come to room temperature and then drizzle it over the top of the ramen bowl just before serving. I like to make a double batch so I have this oil on hand at all times. It is lovely drizzled over a stir-fry or used in salad dressing, too.

1 cup cooking oil

12 scallions, both white and green parts, cut into 2-inch pieces

1. In a small saucepan, heat the oil over medium-high heat. Add the scallions and heat the oil until it begins sizzling. Reduce the heat to low and cook for 30 to 45 minutes, stirring occasionally, until the scallions brown.

2. Strain the oil through a fine-mesh sieve into a mason jar or other heat-safe container. Press down gently on the solids to release as much of the oil as possible. Discard the solids.

STORAGE TIP: Store scallion oil in an airtight container in the refrigerator for up to 3 months.

SESAME-CHILI OIL

5-INGREDIENT, DAIRY-FREE, GLUTEN-FREE, MAKE IT AHEAD, NUT-FREE, VEGAN
PREP TIME: 5 MINUTES, PLUS 20 MINUTES TO COOL / **COOK TIME:** 5 MINUTES
MAKES ABOUT 1 CUP

Chili-infused sesame oil is a spicy condiment with layers of flavor. Just a teaspoonful can completely transform a bowl of ramen, making it spicy but also adding round, toasty, nutty flavor and the bite of fresh ginger.

1 cup sesame oil, divided
2 scallions, white parts only, finely minced

2 tablespoons peeled, minced fresh ginger

2 tablespoons cayenne pepper

1. In a small saucepan, heat ½ cup of oil, the scallions, and the ginger over medium-high heat until sizzling. Simmer, stirring occasionally and reducing the heat if needed to prevent boiling, for 3 minutes.

2. Remove the pan from the heat and transfer the mixture to a heat-safe bowl. Add the cayenne and let the mixture cool to room temperature, about 20 minutes.

3. Stir in the remaining ½ cup of oil and strain the oil into a glass jar.

STORAGE TIP: Store sesame-chili oil in an airtight container in the refrigerator for up to 3 months.

SHICHIMI TOGARASHI

30 MINUTES OR LESS, DAIRY-FREE, GLUTEN-FREE, MAKE IT AHEAD, NUT-FREE, VEGAN

PREP TIME: 5 MINUTES / **COOK TIME:** 5 MINUTES

MAKES ABOUT ¼ CUP

Shichimi togarashi (which means "seven spice") is a mixture that contains dried chiles, dried orange or tangerine zest, sesame seeds, and usually Szechuan peppercorns. It has a spicy kick, layers of nuanced flavor, and a bit of crunch from the crumbled nori and sesame seeds. It is delicious sprinkled onto grilled, broiled, or seared meat or fish. It also elevates a bowl of ramen and gives it kick.

1 tablespoon white sesame seeds

1 tablespoon black sesame seeds

2 teaspoons poppy seeds

1 teaspoon Szechuan peppercorns

2 tablespoons red pepper flakes (preferably Japanese chile)

½ toasted nori sheet

1 tablespoon dried orange or tangerine zest

1. In a small skillet, toast the white and black sesame seeds, poppy seeds, and Szechuan peppercorns over medium-high heat for about 2 minutes, until they begin to pop and become aromatic. Transfer the seeds and peppercorns to a bowl and let them cool for a few minutes.

2. Transfer the mixture to a spice grinder or mortar and pestle and add the red pepper flakes, nori, and zest. Pulse the mixture a few times until coarsely ground (not a fine powder).

STORAGE TIP: Store shichimi togarashi in an airtight container in your spice cabinet for up to 1 month.

*Spicy Miso Ramen
with Crispy
Fried Chicken,* **page 36**

CHAPTER FOUR

CHICKEN RAMEN

These ramen bowls combine the light flavor of a classic chicken-based broth, traditional shio, shoyu, and miso flavorings, and various cuts of chicken (breasts, thighs, and drumsticks) to make some memorable and delicious meals.

These recipes use different cooking methods such as roasting, steaming, braising, and stir-frying. A few of the recipes call for already-cooked chicken. In these cases, I fully endorse buying a rotisserie chicken from the supermarket. Supermarket rotisserie chickens are one of the best shortcuts for a busy home cook. They are almost always succulent and flavorful—and they're ready to eat the minute you get them home. You can also use any cooked chicken you happen to have available.

MISO RAMEN WITH BRAISED CHICKEN THIGHS

DAIRY-FREE, NUT-FREE

PREP TIME: 15 MINUTES, PLUS 30 MINUTES TO MARINATE / **COOK TIME:** 30 MINUTES

SERVES 4

Miso paste gives body and umami flavor to this simple chicken-based ramen. The chicken thighs are marinated first and then braised right in the broth, which adds flavor to the broth and produces tender meat. A light miso is best here, but you can substitute whatever miso paste you have. Bear in mind that the darker the miso paste is, the more intense the flavor will be, so you may want to adjust the quantity.

FOR THE CHICKEN

¼ cup soy sauce or tamari

2 tablespoons mirin

2 teaspoons honey or brown sugar

1 garlic clove, chopped

½ teaspoon peeled, grated fresh ginger

4 boneless, skinless chicken thighs

FOR THE SOUP

1 tablespoon cooking oil

1 small onion, thinly sliced

4 ounces shiitake mushrooms, stemmed and sliced

1 tablespoon peeled, minced fresh ginger

2 garlic cloves, minced

6 cups Basic Chicken Broth (page 9) or store-bought

2 cups water

6 tablespoons miso paste

2 tablespoons sugar

2 tablespoons sake

18 ounces fresh ramen noodles, 12 ounces dried ramen noodles, or 2 packages instant ramen noodles, cooked according to package directions

FOR THE TOPPINGS

1 tablespoon cooking oil

10 leaves chard, center ribs removed, julienned

1 garlic clove, minced

Salt

Freshly ground black pepper

2 Soft-Boiled Eggs (page 27), halved

TO MAKE THE CHICKEN

1. In a medium bowl, combine the soy sauce, mirin, honey, garlic, and ginger, and stir to mix Add the chicken and toss to coat. Refrigerate for at least 30 minutes.

TO MAKE THE SOUP

2. In a stockpot or Dutch oven, heat the oil over medium-high heat. Add the onion and cook for about 5 minutes, stirring occasionally, until the onion is softened. Add the mushrooms and cook, stirring, for 3 minutes more. Stir in the ginger and garlic and then stir in the broth and water. Bring the soup to a simmer.

3. Reduce the heat to medium and add the chicken and marinade to the pot. Simmer, reducing the heat if needed, for 15 to 20 minutes, until the chicken is cooked through.

4. Using a slotted spoon, remove the chicken and transfer it to a bowl. When the chicken is cool enough to handle, slice each thigh, keeping the slices for each thigh together

5. Stir the miso paste, sugar, and sake into the soup and simmer for about 3 minutes, stirring occasionally, until the miso paste is melted and incorporated.

TO MAKE THE TOPPINGS

6. While the soup is cooking, in a skillet heat the oil over medium heat. Add the chard and garlic. Cook for about 4 minutes, stirring, until the chard is wilted and tender. Season the chard with salt and pepper.

7. Divide the noodles among 4 serving bowls and ladle the broth over the noodles. Top each bowl with a sliced chicken thigh, some of the mushrooms, some of the chard, and half an egg. Serve hot.

VARIATION TIP: You can substitute any greens you have for the chard. Spinach, kale, or mustard greens would work just as well.

SPICY MISO RAMEN WITH CRISPY FRIED CHICKEN

DAIRY-FREE, NUT-FREE OPTION

PREP TIME: 15 MINUTES, PLUS 30 MINUTES TO MARINATE / **COOK TIME:** 10 MINUTES

SERVES 4

Crunchy fried chicken pieces are a great textural counterpart to tender noodles and kale. The chicken is deep-fried, but the process is simple. If you want to skip the marinating and frying steps, see the substitution tip at the end of the recipe and feel free to use frozen nuggets instead.

FOR THE CHICKEN

2 tablespoons soy sauce

2 tablespoons sake or mirin

1 teaspoon sesame oil

1 teaspoon peeled, minced fresh ginger

1 teaspoon sugar

¼ teaspoon kosher salt

½ teaspoon freshly ground black pepper

1 pound boneless, skinless chicken thighs, cut into 2-inch pieces

Oil, for frying

½ cup potato starch or cornstarch

FOR THE SOUP

8 cups Basic Chicken Broth (page 9) or store-bought broth

2 teaspoons sesame oil

8 ounces kale leaves, center stems removed and leaves cut into ribbons

½ cup Spicy Miso Tare (page 19)

18 ounces fresh ramen noodles, 12 ounces dried ramen noodles, or 2 packages instant ramen noodles, cooked according to package directions

TO MAKE THE CHICKEN

1. In a medium bowl, stir together the soy sauce, sake, sesame oil, ginger, sugar, salt, and pepper. Add the chicken and stir to coat well. Refrigerate for at least 30 minutes.

2. Fill a saucepan with 2 to 3 inches of oil and heat it over high heat until you can see it shimmering.

3. Remove the chicken pieces from the marinade and discard the marinade.

4. In a bowl, dredge the chicken pieces in the potato starch until they are well coated.

5. Drop the chicken pieces into the hot oil and cook, turning once or twice, until they are golden brown, 3 minutes. Remove the chicken using a slotted spoon and drain it on paper towels.

TO MAKE THE SOUP

6. In a pot, heat the broth over medium-high heat until simmering.

7. While the broth is heating, in a skillet, heat the sesame oil and sauté the kale for about 3 minutes, until it is softened.

8. Into each of 4 serving bowls, put 2 tablespoons of tare. Divide the noodles among the bowls and ladle the broth over the noodles. Arrange the kale and chicken on top. Serve immediately.

SUBSTITUTION TIP: If you don't want to make your own fried chicken pieces, substitute frozen chicken nuggets cooked in the oven until browned and crisp.

MISO RAMEN WITH GARLIC CHICKEN AND SOY SAUCE EGGS

30 MINUTES OR LESS, DAIRY-FREE, NUT-FREE OPTION
PREP TIME: 15 MINUTES / **COOK TIME:** 15 MINUTES
SERVES 4

A quick stir-fried chicken flavored with lots of garlic makes a light but tasty topping for this ramen bowl. Soy sauce eggs add even more flavor and some richness to this otherwise light soup. I love the kick this bowl gets from sliced jalapeño peppers!

FOR THE CHICKEN
2 tablespoons cornstarch
1 teaspoon kosher salt
½ teaspoon freshly ground black pepper
1 pound boneless, skinless chicken thighs, cut into 2-inch pieces
2 tablespoons cooking oil
4 garlic cloves, sliced
2 tablespoons mirin
2 tablespoons soy sauce
¼ teaspoon sugar

FOR THE SOUP
8 cups Basic Chicken Broth (page 9) or store-bought broth
½ cup Basic Miso Tare (page 19)
18 ounces fresh ramen noodles, 12 ounces dried ramen noodles, or 2 packages instant ramen noodles, cooked according to package directions

1 jalapeño, thinly sliced
2 Soy Sauce Eggs (page 28) or Soft-Boiled Eggs (page 27), halved

TO MAKE THE CHICKEN

1. In a medium bowl, whisk the cornstarch, salt, and pepper. Add the chicken pieces and toss to coat them well.

2. In a medium skillet, heat the oil over medium-high heat. Add the chicken pieces and garlic and cook for about 4 minutes, turning the chicken pieces occasionally, until they are golden brown and cooked through.

3. Add the mirin, soy sauce, and sugar, toss to combine, and heat through. Remove the pan from the heat.

TO MAKE THE SOUP

4. In a pot, heat the broth over medium-high heat until simmering.

5. Into each of 4 serving bowls, put 2 tablespoons of tare. Divide the noodles among the bowls and ladle the broth over the noodles. Arrange some of the chicken, a few jalapeño slices, and half an egg on top of each bowl. Serve immediately.

INGREDIENT TIP: Soy Sauce Eggs make a great ramen topping, but they are also great for snacking on.

MISO-GINGER RAMEN WITH CHICKEN AND BLACKENED LEMONS

30 MINUTES OR LESS, DAIRY-FREE, GLUTEN-FREE (USE GLUTEN-FREE NOODLES), NUT-FREE OPTION

PREP TIME: 15 MINUTES / **COOK TIME:** 10 MINUTES

SERVES 4

This is a really simple recipe, but adding charred lemon halves gives it a bit of drama. The blackened lemon also adds some nice citrus and smoky notes to the soup. You can make this using either leftover cooked chicken or rotisserie chicken from the supermarket.

8 cups **Basic Chicken Broth** (page 9) **or** store-bought broth

2 small lemons, washed well, halved, and visible seeds removed

½ cup **Basic Miso Tare** (page 19)

2 teaspoons peeled, grated fresh ginger

18 ounces fresh ramen noodles, 12 ounces dried ramen noodles, or 2 packages instant ramen noodles, cooked according to package directions

12 ounces cooked, shredded chicken

1. In a pot, heat the broth over medium-high heat until simmering.

2. Heat a grill or skillet over high heat. Place the lemons cut-side down on the grill or skillet. Cook for 3 to 5 minutes, until the lemons are heated through and charred on the cut sides. Ideally, you'll cook them without moving them so they char nicely, but if the heat seems uneven, adjust them so they char evenly.

3. In a small bowl, stir together the miso tare and ginger.

4. Into each of 4 serving bowls, put 2 tablespoons of the tare-ginger mixture. Divide the noodles among the bowls and ladle the broth over the noodles. Arrange some of the chicken and a charred lemon half on top of each bowl. Serve immediately. Diners can squeeze the lemon into the broth for added flavor.

SUBSTITUTION TIP: If you have access to Meyer lemons, use those for this recipe. They are less tart than regular lemons, but more fragrant.

SHIO RAMEN WITH GINGER CHICKEN AND BOK CHOY

DAIRY-FREE, NUT-FREE

PREP TIME: 15 MINUTES, PLUS 15 MINUTES TO MARINATE / **COOK TIME:** 10 MINUTES

SERVES 4

This simple ramen is topped with gingery stir-fried chicken. It's quick to make, but if you take the time to marinate the chicken (for anywhere from 15 minutes to overnight), it will be even more flavorful.

FOR THE CHICKEN

2 tablespoons soy sauce

2 tablespoons sake

2 tablespoons honey

1 tablespoon peeled, grated fresh ginger

1 pound boneless, skinless chicken thighs, cut into bite-size pieces

1 tablespoon cooking oil

FOR THE SOUP

8 cups Basic Chicken Broth (page 9) or store-bought broth

8 to 12 baby bok choy

½ cup Basic Shio Tare (page 17)

18 ounces fresh ramen noodles, 12 ounces dried ramen noodles, or 2 packages instant ramen noodles, cooked according to package directions

8 ounces fresh shiitake mushrooms, sliced

TO MAKE THE CHICKEN

1. In a medium bowl, whisk together the soy sauce, sake, honey, and ginger. Add the chicken pieces and toss to coat them well. Marinate the chicken for 15 to 20 minutes.

2. In a medium skillet, heat the oil over medium-high heat. Add the chicken to the pan, discarding the marinade, and cook, stirring occasionally, until the chicken is cooked through and golden brown, 4 minutes.

CONTINUED

TO MAKE THE SOUP

3. In a pot, heat the broth over medium-high heat until simmering. Add the bok choy and cook for 3 to 4 minutes, until wilted.

4. Into each of 4 serving bowls, put 2 tablespoons of tare. Divide the noodles among the bowls and ladle the broth over the noodles. Divide the bok choy, chicken, and mushrooms among the bowls and serve immediately.

SUBSTITUTION TIP: This ramen combination would work equally well with a miso seasoning base. Just substitute Basic Miso Tare (page 19), or the spicy variation of it, for the shio tare.

SPICY CHICKEN RAMEN WITH CHILES AND BASIL

30 MINUTES OR LESS, DAIRY-FREE, NUT-FREE
PREP TIME: 15 MINUTES / **COOK TIME:** 5 MINUTES
SERVES 4

I love adding fresh herbs and chiles to a bowl of ramen. They're simple ingredients that require very little prep, but they provide a real boost of fresh flavor. You can use milder chiles like red jalapeños or spicier ones like red serrano chiles.

1 tablespoon sesame oil
2 teaspoons peeled, grated fresh ginger
1 garlic clove, minced
1 pound ground chicken
1 tablespoon soy sauce
1 teaspoon chili oil
8 cups Basic Chicken Broth (page 9) **or store-bought broth**

½ cup Basic Shio Tare (page 17)
18 ounces fresh ramen noodles, 12 ounces dried ramen noodles, or 2 packages instant ramen noodles, cooked according to package directions

¼ cup thinly sliced fresh basil
2 fresh red chiles, thinly sliced

1. In a medium skillet, heat the sesame oil over medium-high heat. Add the ginger and garlic and cook, stirring, for about 30 seconds, until fragrant. Add the chicken and cook for about 4 minutes, stirring, until it is cooked through. Stir in the soy sauce and chili oil.

2. In a pot, heat the broth over medium-high heat until simmering.

3. Into each of 4 serving bowls, put 2 tablespoons of tare. Divide the noodles among the bowls and ladle the broth over the noodles. Divide the chicken and basil among the bowls and arrange a few of the chile slices on each. Serve immediately.

COOKING TIP: Wear rubber gloves when handling fresh chiles to protect your hands from the capsaicin oil, which can irritate the skin and be transferred to your eyes or lips when you touch your face.

SHIO PHO (VIENAMESE-STYLE SHREDDED-CHICKEN RAMEN)

30 MINUTES OR LESS, DAIRY-FREE, NUT-FREE
PREP TIME: 15 MINUTES / **COOK TIME:** 5 MINUTES
SERVES 4

This ramen, inspired by the flavors of the Vietnamese beef noodle soup pho, is as easy to make as heating broth, cooking noodles, and slicing some fresh herbs and chiles. I like to use a rotisserie chicken for this, but you can use any leftover cooked chicken you have.

8 cups **Basic Chicken Broth** (page 9) **or** store-bought broth
½ cup **Basic Shio Tare** (page 17)

18 ounces fresh ramen noodles, 12 ounces dried ramen noodles, or 2 packages instant ramen noodles, cooked according to package directions

12 ounces cooked, shredded chicken
1 cup bean sprouts
1 cup fresh cilantro leaves
1 jalapeño pepper, thinly sliced
1 lime, quartered

1. To make the soup, heat the broth over medium-high heat until simmering.

2. Into each of 4 serving bowls, put 2 tablespoons of tare. Divide the noodles among the bowls and ladle the broth over the noodles. Divide the chicken, bean sprouts, cilantro, and chile slices among the bowls.

3. Serve immediately, with lime wedges to be squeezed into the soup just before eating.

VARIATION TIP: For added Vietnamese flavor, toss a dried star anise pod or two into the broth while it simmers. It adds a subtle licorice flavor that is distinctly Vietnamese.

SHOYU RAMEN WITH PANKO-BREADED CHICKEN AND SPINACH

30 MINUTES OR LESS, DAIRY-FREE, NUT-FREE
PREP TIME: 15 MINUTES / **COOK TIME:** 15 MINUTES
SERVES 4

Panko are Japanese-style bread crumbs that are widely available in supermarkets in the United States. They are crisper and lighter than regular bread crumbs. Used as breading for crispy oven-fried chicken tenders, they add a really nice textural contrast in this simple bowl of ramen.

1 pound chicken
  breast tenders
½ teaspoon kosher salt
½ teaspoon freshly
  ground black pepper
1 cup panko
  bread crumbs
1 large egg, beaten
8 cups Basic Chicken
  Broth (page 9) or
  store-bought broth

½ cup Basic Shoyu Tare
  (page 18)
18 ounces fresh ramen
  noodles, 12 ounces
  dried ramen noodles,
  or 2 packages instant
  ramen noodles,
  cooked according to
  package directions

6 cups fresh spinach
  leaves, blanched in
  boiling water or wilted
  in a nonstick pan
4 teaspoons sesame oil

1. Preheat the oven to 375°F, line a baking sheet with parchment paper or aluminum foil, and set it aside.

2. Season the chicken pieces with the salt and pepper.

3. Put the panko in a shallow bowl and the egg in a separate shallow bowl.

4. Dunk the chicken pieces first in the egg and then in the panko, turning to make sure each piece is well coated.

CONTINUED

5. Arrange the chicken pieces on the prepared baking sheet. Bake for 13 to 15 minutes, until golden brown, crisp on the outside, and cooked through.

6. In a pot, heat the broth over medium-high heat until simmering.

7. Into each of 4 serving bowls, put 2 tablespoons of tare. Divide the noodles among the bowls and ladle the broth over the noodles. Divide the chicken and spinach among the bowls. Drizzle 1 teaspoon of sesame oil over each bowl and serve immediately.

SUBSTITUTION TIP: If you don't want to bother with cooking your own crispy chicken strips, you can buy them frozen. Heat them as directed on the package until they are golden brown and crisp.

SHOYU RAMEN WITH SAKE-STEAMED CHICKEN DRUMSTICKS

DAIRY-FREE, NUT-FREE

PREP TIME: 10 MINUTES, PLUS 15 MINUTES TO MARINATE / **COOK TIME:** 20 MINUTES

SERVES 4

Steaming chicken in sake infuses it with flavor and leaves the meat perfectly tender. It's the perfect preparation for ramen. A citrus-soy sauce adds a boost of bright flavor.

¾ cup sake

¾ cup water

4 chicken drumsticks

Kosher salt

1 tablespoon soy sauce

1 tablespoon freshly squeezed orange juice

2 teaspoons rice vinegar

2 teaspoons peeled, minced fresh ginger

1 teaspoon mirin

1 garlic clove, minced

8 cups Basic Chicken Broth (page 9) or store-bought broth

½ cup Basic Shoyu Tare (page 18)

18 ounces fresh ramen noodles, 12 ounces dried ramen noodles, or 2 packages instant ramen noodles, cooked according to package directions

3 scallions, both white and green parts, thinly sliced

1. In a stockpot or large saucepan, place a steamer basket. Put the sake and water in the pot and bring the liquid to a boil.

2. Season the drumsticks generously with salt and place them in the steamer basket. Cover the pot and reduce the heat to low. Steam the chicken for about 20 minutes, until it is cooked through.

3. In a medium bowl, combine the soy sauce, orange juice, vinegar, ginger, mirin, and garlic, and stir to mix. Add the chicken to the bowl and toss to coat. Let it stand for 15 minutes while you prepare the soup.

4. To make the soup, heat the broth over medium-high heat until simmering.

5. Into each of 4 serving bowls, put 2 tablespoons of tare. Divide the noodles among the bowls and ladle the broth over the noodles. Arrange a drumstick and scallions on top of each bowl. Serve immediately.

SUBSTITUTION TIP: Use baked or roasted chicken drumsticks if you like. Toss the drumsticks in the sauce while they are still hot to infuse with flavor.

SHOYU CHICKEN RAMEN WITH MISO-GLAZED CARROTS

30 MINUTES OR LESS, DAIRY-FREE, NUT-FREE
PREP TIME: 10 MINUTES / **COOK TIME:** 10 MINUTES
SERVES 4

Red miso paste is intensely salty and rich with umami. Here it cooks down to a glaze that coats the carrots, making them irresistible.

2 teaspoons sesame oil

2 cups sliced carrots

½ cup water

2 teaspoons red
   miso paste

1 teaspoon peeled,
   grated fresh ginger

Kosher salt

8 cups Basic Chicken
   Broth (page 9)
   or store-bought
   chicken broth

½ cup **Basic Shoyu Tare**
   (page 18)

18 ounces fresh ramen
   noodles, 12 ounces
   dried ramen noodles,
   or 2 packages instant
   ramen noodles,
   cooked according to
   package directions

12 ounces cooked,
   shredded chicken

2 tablespoons
   chopped chives

1. In a skillet, heat the sesame oil over medium-high heat. Add the carrots and cook for about 5 minutes, stirring occasionally, until they begin to soften.

2. In small bowl, whisk together the water, miso paste, and ginger until well combined. Add the mixture to the skillet with the carrots, reduce the heat to low, and simmer for about 5 minutes, until the carrots are tender and the liquid has reduced to a glaze. Season with salt.

3. To make the soup, heat the broth over medium-high heat until simmering.

4. Into each of 4 serving bowls, put 2 tablespoons of tare. Divide the noodles among the bowls and ladle the broth over the noodles. Divide the chicken, carrots, and chives on top of each bowl. Serve immediately.

VARIATION TIP: Try using other root vegetables—parsnips, turnips, or a daikon radish will be great too.

SHOYU RAMEN WITH CRISPY CHICKEN STRIPS

30 MINUTES OR LESS, DAIRY-FREE, NUT-FREE
PREP TIME: 10 MINUTES / **COOK TIME:** 15 MINUTES
SERVES 4

I just can't get enough of the combination of crispy chicken and soft-boiled eggs in a bowl of ramen. Nori strips add some welcome green to the bowl, and they're easy to keep in your pantry so you always have them on hand.

1 pound chicken breast tenders

½ teaspoon kosher salt

½ teaspoon freshly ground black pepper

1 large egg, beaten

1 cup panko bread crumbs

8 cups Basic Chicken Broth (page 9) or store-bought broth

½ cup Basic Shoyu Tare (page 18)

18 ounces fresh ramen noodles, 12 ounces dried ramen noodles, or 2 packages instant ramen noodles, cooked according to package directions

1 sheet nori, cut into 3-inch strips

2 Soft-Boiled Eggs (page 27), **halved**

1. Preheat the oven to 375°F and line a baking sheet with parchment paper or aluminum foil.

2. Season the chicken pieces with the salt and pepper.

3. Place the egg in a shallow bowl and the panko in another shallow bowl.

4. Dunk the chicken pieces first in the egg and then in the panko, turning to make sure each piece is well coated.

5. Arrange the chicken pieces on the prepared baking sheet. Bake for 13 to 15 minutes, until golden brown and crisp on the outside and cooked through.

CONTINUED

6. To make the soup, heat the broth over medium-high heat until simmering.

7. Into each of 4 serving bowls, put 2 tablespoons of tare. Divide the noodles among the bowls and ladle the broth over the noodles. Divide the chicken and nori strips among the bowls and top each bowl with half an egg. Serve immediately.

VARIATION TIP: If you don't mind a tiny bit of extra cooking, you can substitute sautéed chard or kale for the nori strips.

Shio Ramen with Crispy Pork Belly, Scallions, Seasoned Bamboo Shoots, and Nori, **page 65**

CHAPTER FIVE

PORK RAMEN

From the intensely rich tonkotsu pork broth to the classic chashu pork topping, pork is one of the most common ingredients in a bowl of ramen. The recipes here utilize different cuts and styles of pork, from a pork-based broth to pork loin, succulent pork belly, crispy bacon, shredded pork shoulder, and even Spam.

When you're using rich cuts of pork, you can still create a nuanced bowl of ramen with both intense and delicate flavors. Adding fresh herbs like cilantro and scallions, leafy greens like chard, kale, and bok choy, and flavorful finishes like crushed peanuts, Sesame-Chili Oil (page 30), or Scallion Oil (page 29) keeps these bowls from being overwhelmed by the meat.

SPICY MISO RAMEN WITH GRILLED PORK TENDERLOIN

DAIRY-FREE

PREP TIME: 15 MINUTES, PLUS 8 HOURS TO MARINATE / **COOK TIME:** 15 MINUTES

SERVES 4

The pork tenderloin is marinated in a savory blend of miso paste, soy sauce, rice wine, and sesame oil, then grilled. The rich pork broth–based ramen uses Spicy Miso Tare as the seasoning, which is rich and flavorful.

FOR THE PORK

1½ tablespoons sugar

1½ tablespoons miso paste (white or red)

1½ tablespoons soy sauce

1½ tablespoons mirin

1½ tablespoons sesame oil

1½ tablespoons toasted sesame seeds

1 tablespoon rice vinegar

2 garlic cloves, minced

1 pound pork tenderloin

FOR THE SOUP

2 teaspoons sesame oil

8 ounces kale leaves, center stems removed and leaves cut into ribbons

8 cups Basic Pork Broth (page 10) or store-bought broth

½ cup Spicy Miso Tare (page 19)

18 ounces fresh ramen noodles, 12 ounces dried ramen noodles, or 2 packages instant ramen noodles, cooked according to package directions

½ cup chopped scallions

TO MAKE THE PORK

1. In a medium bowl, combine the sugar, miso paste, soy sauce, mirin, sesame oil, sesame seeds, vinegar, and garlic. Add the pork and turn to coat. Cover and refrigerate for 8 hours or overnight.

2. Heat a grill or grill pan to medium-high heat. Grill the pork loin for 8 to 10 minutes total, turning every few minutes, until cooked through.

3. Remove the meat from the grill and let it stand for 10 minutes before slicing it thinly.

TO MAKE THE SOUP

4. In a medium skillet, heat the sesame oil over medium-high heat. Add the kale and cook for 3 to 5 minutes, stirring, until tender.

5. In a pot, heat the broth over medium-high heat until simmering.

6. Into each of 4 serving bowls, put 2 tablespoons of tare. Divide the noodles among the bowls and ladle the broth over the noodles. Divide the pork slices atop the noodles. Garnish with the scallions. Serve immediately.

SUBSTITUTION TIP: If you don't have pork broth, you can use chicken broth instead. The flavor will be a bit lighter, but still delicious

MISO RAMEN WITH STIR-FRIED GINGER PORK AND GREENS

30 MINUTES OR LESS, DAIRY-FREE, NUT-FREE OPTION
PREP TIME: 10 MINUTES / **COOK TIME:** 10 MINUTES
SERVES 4

Ground pork makes this ramen easy to prepare and on the table in 20 minutes. First you stir-fry the pork with fragrant ginger and seasonings, then you stir-fry the greens in the same skillet, and then you warm the broth. Topped with a drizzle of scallion oil to amp up the flavor even more, this is a perfect meal for a busy weeknight.

FOR THE PORK

1 pound ground pork
½ teaspoon kosher salt
2-inch piece fresh ginger, peeled and minced
1 teaspoon soy sauce

FOR THE GREENS

1 tablespoon cooking oil
10 leaves kale or chard, thick center stems removed and leaves julienned
1 garlic clove, minced

FOR THE SOUP

8 cups Basic Pork Broth (page 10) or store-bought broth
½ cup Basic Miso Tare (page 19)
18 ounces fresh ramen noodles, 12 ounces dried ramen noodles, or 2 packages instant ramen noodles, cooked according to package directions
4 teaspoons Scallion Oil (page 29)

TO MAKE THE PORK

1. In a large skillet over medium heat, cook the pork. Season the pork with the salt and cook for 5 minutes, stirring and breaking up the meat with a spatula, until browned. Add the ginger and cook, stirring, for 1 minute more. Remove the skillet from the heat and stir in the soy sauce. Transfer the pork mixture to a bowl and set it aside.

TO MAKE THE GREENS

2. In the same skillet (wipe it out first), heat the oil over medium-high heat. Add the greens and cook, stirring, until wilted, 4 minutes. Stir in the garlic and cook for 1 minute more.

TO MAKE THE SOUP

3. In a pot, heat the broth over medium-high heat until simmering.

4. Into each of 4 serving bowls, put 2 tablespoons of tare. Divide the noodles among the bowls and ladle the broth over the noodles. Divide the pork and greens among the bowls. Drizzle 1 teaspoon of scallion oil over each bowl. Serve immediately.

SUBSTITUTION TIP: If you don't have scallion oil, substitute sesame oil or Sesame-Chili Oil (page 30).

MISO RAMEN WITH CRISPY BACON AND ROASTED TOMATOES

30 MINUTES OR LESS, DAIRY-FREE, GLUTEN-FREE (USE GLUTEN-FREE NOODLES), NUT-FREE OPTION

PREP TIME: 10 MINUTES / **COOK TIME:** 5 MINUTES

SERVES 4

Ivan Orkin is Japan's only American-born ramen master; he has opened ramen restaurants in both New York and Tokyo. One of Orkin's signature moves is adding roasted tomatoes to his ramen bowls. The tomatoes add a deep, rich, sweet-tart note and exemplify why using local ingredients in ramen is always fair game. This bowl combines smoky American-style bacon with roasted tomatoes for an unexpected yet decidedly delicious twist on ramen.

8 cups Basic Chicken Broth (page 9) **or store-bought broth**

½ cup Basic Miso Tare (page 19)

18 ounces fresh ramen noodles, 12 ounces dried ramen noodles, or 2 packages instant ramen noodles, cooked according to package directions

4 bacon strips, cooked until crisp

4 Roasted Tomatoes (oage 24)**, cut into halves**

4 scallions, both white and green parts, thinly sliced

1. To make the soup, heat the broth over medium-high heat until simmering.

2. Into each of 4 serving bowls, put 2 tablespoons of tare. Divide the noodles among the bowls and ladle the broth over the noodles. Arrange 1 strip of bacon and 2 tomato halves on top of each bowl. Garnish with the scallions. Serve immediately.

SUBSTITUTION TIP: If you don't have bacon, you can substitute pancetta, crispy pork belly, Canadian bacon, or ham.

MISO RAMEN WITH CRISPY TONKATSU AND CABBAGE

30 MINUTES OR LESS, DAIRY-FREE
PREP TIME: 15 MINUTES / **COOK TIME:** 10 MINUTES
SERVES 4

Tonkatsu (not to be confused with tonkotsu, which is pork broth) refers to a pork loin cutlet that is coated in crispy panko bread crumbs and deep-fried. It is typically served over rice, but it also makes a perfect topping for a bowl of miso ramen. Tonkatsu sauce is a sweet and savory condiment made from fruits and vegetables. You can buy tonkatsu sauce in Japanese or Asian markets or in many supermarkets.

FOR THE PORK
4 (¼-inch-thick) slices
   pork loin
Kosher salt
Freshly ground
   black pepper
¼ cup all-purpose flour
1 large egg, lightly beaten
1 cup panko
   bread crumbs
Vegetable oil,
   for panfrying

FOR THE SOUP
8 cups Basic Pork
   Broth (page 10) or
   store-bought broth
½ cup Basic Miso Tare
   (page 19)

18 ounces fresh ramen
   noodles, 12 ounces
   dried ramen noodles,
   or 2 packages instant
   ramen noodles,
   cooked according to
   package directions
2 cups shredded cabbage
¼ cup tonkatsu sauce

TO MAKE THE PORK

1. Season the pork on both sides with salt and pepper. Put the flour, the egg, and the panko in separate shallow bowls. Dredge each pork slice in the flour, coating both sides. Dunk the dredged slices in the egg and then in the panko to coat.

CONTINUED

2. Fill a skillet about ½ inch deep with cooking oil. Heat the oil over medium-high heat until it shimmers. Add the breaded pork and cook for 6 to 7 minutes, turning once, until golden brown and crisp on both sides. You may have to cook the cutlets in two batches unless you use a large skillet. Transfer the cooked pieces to a paper towel–lined plate to drain.

3. Once they have cooled slightly, cut the pork cutlets into strips.

TO MAKE THE SOUP

4. In a pot, heat the broth over medium-high heat until simmering.

5. Into each of 4 serving bowls, put 2 tablespoons of tare. Divide the noodles among the bowls and ladle the broth over the noodles. Arrange the cooked pork and shredded cabbage on top of each bowl, dividing them equally. Drizzle the sauce over the tonkatsu and serve immediately.

COOKING TIP: In Japan, tonkatsu is often double fried to make the coating extra crisp. To replicate that at home, after frying the first time as directed, let the cutlets cool for several minutes and then return them to the hot oil and fry a second time for 2 to 3 minutes.

SHIO RAMEN WITH SHREDDED PORK AND SESAME-CHILI OIL

DAIRY-FREE, NUT-FREE

PREP TIME: 15 MINUTES / **COOK TIME:** 6 HOURS (SLOW COOKER) OR 1 HOUR (PRESSURE COOKER)

SERVES 4

This Japanese-style shredded pork is simple to make, either in a slow cooker or a pressure cooker, and the result is melt-in-your-mouth tender and full of flavor. The pork is slightly sweet, so a drizzle of sesame-chili oil balances it with a little kick of heat. This recipe makes more pork than you will need for this soup. You can use the same pork to make the Shoyu Ramen with Crispy Shredded Pork and Arugula (page 70). Store any extra pork in the refrigerator for up to 3 days or in the freezer for up to 3 months.

FOR THE PORK

- 1 (3½- to 4-pound) pork shoulder, cut into a few large pieces
- 1 teaspoon kosher salt
- 1 cup water
- 1 onion, diced
- ½ cup soy sauce
- ¼ cup sake
- ¼ cup brown sugar
- 6 garlic cloves, minced
- 1-inch piece fresh ginger, peeled and sliced

FOR THE SOUP

- 8 cups Basic Pork Broth (page 13) or store-bought broth
- ½ cup Basic Shio Tare (page 17)
- 18 ounces fresh ramen noodles, 12 ounces dried ramen noodles, or 2 packages instant ramen noodles, cooked according to package directions
- 4 scallions, both white and green parts, thinly sliced
- 4 teaspoons Sesame-Chili Oil (page 30) or store-bought chili oil

TO MAKE THE PORK

1. Put the pork into a slow cooker or pressure cooker, and season it all over with the salt.

2. In a medium bowl, stir together the water, onion, soy sauce, sake, sugar, garlic, and ginger. Pour the mixture over the meat.

CONTINUED

3. If using a slow cooker, cover and cook on high for 6 hours. If using a pressure cooker, cover, turn the valve to the sealing position, and pressure cook for 1 hour. When the cooking time is up, let the pressure release naturally.

4. When the meat is cooked, it should be very tender and shred easily with a fork. Transfer the meat to a medium bowl and let it rest for 15 minutes or so before shredding it with two forks.

TO MAKE THE SOUP

5. In a pot, heat the broth over medium-high heat until simmering.

6. Into each of 4 serving bowls, put 2 tablespoons of tare. Divide the noodles among the bowls and ladle the broth over the noodles. Pile some of the cooked pork on top of each bowl and top it with the scallions. Drizzle 1 teaspoon of chili oil over each bowl and serve immediately.

VARIATION TIP: If you don't have a slow cooker or pressure cooker, you can cook the meat in a Dutch oven on the stove. Add everything to the Dutch oven and bring the ingredients to a simmer over medium-high heat. Reduce the heat to medium-low, cover the pot, and simmer for about 2½ hours, until the meat falls apart easily.

SHIO RAMEN WITH SESAME-GINGER PORK AND BABY BOK CHOY

30 MINUTES OR LESS, DAIRY-FREE, NUT-FREE
PREP TIME: 15 MINUTES / **COOK TIME:** 10 MINUTES
SERVES 4

This is another simple ramen bowl that comes together almost effortlessly. Ground pork is quickly stir-fried with ginger, sesame, and other seasonings. The baby bok choy cooks in the broth while it is being heated.

FOR THE PORK

1 pound ground pork

½ teaspoon kosher salt

2-inch piece fresh ginger, peeled and minced

1 tablespoon Japanese sesame paste

1 teaspoon soy sauce

FOR THE SOUP

8 cups Basic Pork Broth (page 10) or store-bought broth

12 baby bok choy

½ cup Basic Shio Tare (page 17)

18 ounces fresh ramen noodles, 12 ounces dried ramen noodles, or 2 packages instant ramen noodles, cooked according to package directions

4 scallions, both white and green parts, thinly sliced

TO MAKE THE PORK

1. In a large skillet, heat the pork over medium-high heat. Season it with salt and cook for 5 minutes, stirring and breaking up the meat with a spatula, until browned. Add the ginger and cook, stirring, for 1 minute more, until fragrant. Remove the skillet from the heat and stir in the sesame paste and soy sauce.

TO MAKE THE SOUP

2. In a pot, heat the broth over medium-high heat until simmering. Add the bok choy and cook for 3 to 4 minutes, until wilted.

CONTINUED

3. Into each of 4 serving bowls, put 2 tablespoons of tare. Divide the noodles among the bowls and ladle the broth over the noodles. Divide the pork, bok choy, and scallions among the bowls. Serve immediately.

SUBSTITUTION TIP: If you don't have Japanese or Chinese sesame paste, you can substitute creamy, no-sugar-added peanut butter or sesame oil. I don't recommend using tahini because the taste and texture are both different.

SHIO RAMEN WITH CRISPY PORK BELLY, SCALLIONS, SEASONED BAMBOO SHOOTS, AND NORI

DAIRY-FREE, NUT-FREE
PREP TIME: 15 MINUTES / **COOK TIME:** 2 HOURS 45 MINUTES
SERVES 4

Crispy slices of rich, flavorful pork belly make the perfect topping for a sumptuous bowl of ramen. The pork belly is easy to roast in the oven, but it does take a few hours. Plan to spend a weekend afternoon hanging around the kitchen while it cooks. It will be time well spent.

FOR THE PORK
1 pound pork
   belly, skin-on
1 tablespoon cooking oil
Kosher salt
Freshly ground
   black pepper

FOR THE SOUP
8 cups Basic Pork
   Broth (page 10) or
   store-bought broth
½ cup Basic Shio Tare
   (page 17)
18 ounces fresh ramen
   noodles, 12 ounces
   dried ramen noodles,
   or 2 packages instant
   ramen noodles,
   cooked according to
   package directions

4 scallions, both white
   and green parts,
   thinly sliced
½ cup Seasoned
   Bamboo Shoots
   (page 22) or canned
   sliced bamboo shoots
1 sheet nori, cut
   into strips

TO MAKE THE PORK

1. Preheat the oven to 350°F and put a wire rack on top of a baking sheet.

2. Score the skin of the pork belly with a very sharp knife, making several small cuts into the skin and fat layer without puncturing the meat. Rub the oil all over the meat and then season it generously with salt and pepper.

3. Place the meat on the rack on top of the baking sheet, skin-side up, and roast for 2½ hours.

CONTINUED

4. Raise the heat to 450°F and roast for 15 minutes more.

5. Remove the meat from the oven and let it stand for 15 minutes. Cut the cooked pork belly into ¼-inch-thick slices.

TO MAKE THE SOUP

6. In a pot, heat the broth over medium-high heat until simmering.

7. Into each of 4 serving bowls, put 2 tablespoons of tare. Divide the noodles among the bowls and ladle the broth over the noodles. Divide the pork, scallions, bamboo shoots, and nori strips among the bowls. Serve immediately.

COOKING TIP: To make scoring the skin of the pork easier, chill the meat very well beforehand. You may even want to put it in the freezer for 30 minutes or so.

SHIO RAMEN WITH HAM AND SHIITAKE MUSHROOMS

30 MINUTES OR LESS, DAIRY-FREE, GLUTEN-FREE (USE GLUTEN-FREE NOODLES), NUT-FREE

PREP TIME: 10 MINUTES / **COOK TIME:** 10 MINUTES
SERVES 4

Ramen is a great way to use up leftovers in your refrigerator. I love to make this version whenever I have ham left over after a holiday meal, like at Christmas or Easter. Since the ham is already cooked, this soup can be tossed together in minutes.

8 cups Basic Pork Broth (page 10) **or store-bought broth**
2 teaspoons cooking oil
12 ounces thickly sliced cooked ham, diced
4 ounces shiitake mushrooms, sliced
Pinch salt

½ cup Basic Shio Tare (page 17)
18 ounces fresh ramen noodles, 12 ounces dried ramen noodles, or 2 packages instant ramen noodles, cooked according to package directions

4 scallions, both white and green parts, thinly sliced
2 Soft-Boiled Eggs (page 27), **halved**

1. In a stockpot, heat the broth over medium-high heat until simmering.

2. In a medium skillet, heat the oil over medium-high heat. Add the ham and cook for 4 minutes, stirring occasionally, until heated through and browned in spots. Transfer the ham to a bowl or plate.

3. In the same skillet, cook the mushrooms with a pinch of salt for 3 to 4 minutes, stirring occasionally, until tender.

4. Into each of 4 serving bowls, put 2 tablespoons of tare. Divide the noodles among the bowls and ladle the broth over the noodles. Divide the ham, mushrooms, and scallions among the bowls and place half an egg on top of each bowl. Serve immediately.

SUBSTITUTION TIP: If you don't have thickly sliced ham, you can use deli-sliced ham cut into strips. This type of ham will only take 1 or 2 minutes to heat up in a hot skillet.

SHOYU PORK RAMEN WITH SLICED PORK LOIN AND SHRIMP

DAIRY-FREE, NUT-FREE

PREP TIME: 10 MINUTES, PLUS 30 MINUTES TO MARINATE / **COOK TIME:** 10 MINUTES

SERVES 4

Shrimp and pork are a great pair for topping a bowl of ramen. Here the pork's flavor is amped up by cooking it with fresh ginger and tender shiitake mushrooms. I like to finish the bowl off with a drizzle of Scallion Oil (page 29) when I have it on hand.

FOR THE PORK

3 tablespoons soy sauce

1½ tablespoons sake

1 teaspoon sugar

1 teaspoon peeled, minced fresh ginger

4 (¼-inch-thick) slices pork loin

1 tablespoon cooking oil

4 ounces shiitake mushrooms, sliced

FOR THE SOUP

8 cups Basic Pork Broth (page 10) or store-bought broth

½ cup Basic Shoyu Tare (page 18)

18 ounces fresh ramen noodles, 12 ounces dried ramen noodles, or 2 packages instant ramen noodles, cooked according to package directions

12 cooked shrimp

4 scallions, both white and green parts, thinly sliced

TO MAKE THE PORK

1. In a medium bowl, stir together the soy sauce, sake, sugar, and ginger. Add the pork and toss to coat. Cover the bowl and refrigerate the pork and marinade for at least 30 minutes.

2. In a large skillet, heat the oil over medium-high heat. Remove the pork slices from the marinade, reserving the marinade, and place them in the pan. Cook for about 4 minutes, until browned on the bottom. Flip the pork slices over, add the mushrooms to the pan, and cook for about 4 minutes more, until the second side of the pork is browned and the pork is cooked through.

3. Add the reserved marinade to the pan, raise the heat to high, and bring to a boil. Cook for 2 to 3 minutes more, basting the meat with the liquid, until the liquid begins to thicken.

TO MAKE THE SOUP

4. In a pot, heat the broth over medium-high heat until simmering.

5. Into each of 4 serving bowls, put 2 tablespoons of tare. Divide the noodles among the bowls and ladle the broth over the noodles. Arrange a pork slice on each bowl and divide the mushrooms, shrimp, and scallions among the bowls. Drizzle some of the pan sauce from the pork over the top of each bowl and serve immediately.

SUBSTITUTION TIP: If you have raw shrimp, drop it into the simmering broth and cook for 2 to 3 minutes, just until it is opaque and cooked through.

SHOYU RAMEN WITH CRISPY SHREDDED PORK AND ARUGULA

DAIRY-FREE, NUT-FREE

PREP TIME: 15 MINUTES / **COOK TIME:** 6 HOURS 10 MINUTES (SLOW COOKER) OR 1 HOUR AND 10 MINUTES (PRESSURE COOKER)

SERVES 4

I love the contrast of the rich pork and the spicy fresh arugula here. The pork used here is the same as the pork in Shio Ramen with Shredded Pork and Sesame-Chili Oil (page 61), but in this recipe, it is crisped under the broiler to finish it. You won't use the full amount of pork here, but you can store the extra in the refrigerator for up to 3 days or in the freezer for up to 3 months. Serve it over steamed rice or use it in another ramen meal.

FOR THE PORK

1 (3½- to 4-pound) pork shoulder, cut into a few large pieces

1 teaspoon kosher salt

1 cup water

1 onion, diced

½ cup soy sauce

¼ cup sake

¼ cup brown sugar

6 garlic cloves, minced

1-inch piece fresh ginger, peeled and sliced

FOR THE SOUP

8 cups Basic Pork Broth (page 10) or store-bought broth

½ cup Basic Shoyu Tare (page 18)

18 ounces fresh ramen noodles, 12 ounces dried ramen noodles, or 2 packages instant ramen noodles, cooked according to package directions

4 cups arugula

2 Soft-Boiled Eggs (page 27), halved

4 scallions, both white and green parts, thinly sliced

TO MAKE THE PORK

1. Into a slow cooker or pressure cooker, put the pork and season the meat all over with salt.

2. In a medium bowl, stir together the water, onion, soy sauce, sake, brown sugar, garlic, and ginger. Pour the mixture over the meat.

3. If using a slow cooker, cover and cook on high for 6 hours. If using a pressure cooker, cover, turn the valve to the sealing position, and pressure cook for 1 hour. When the cooking time is up, let the pressure release naturally.

4. When the meat is cooked, it should be very tender and shred easily with a fork. Transfer the meat to a medium bowl and let it rest for 15 minutes or so before shredding it with two forks.

5. Spread the meat out on a baking sheet and cook under the broiler for 4 to 6 minutes, until it crisps up.

TO MAKE THE SOUP

6. In a pot, heat the broth over medium-high heat until simmering.

7. Into each of 4 serving bowls, put 2 tablespoons of tare. Divide the noodles among the bowls and ladle the broth over the noodles. Pile some of the cooked pork, 1 cup of arugula, and half an egg on top of each bowl and top with the scallions. Serve immediately.

SUBSTITUTION TIP: If you don't have arugula, substitute fresh baby spinach leaves or any baby salad greens.

SHOYU RAMEN WITH BACON, SOFT-BOILED EGGS, AND CRISPY KALE

30 MINUTES OR LESS, DAIRY-FREE, NUT-FREE
PREP TIME: 10 MINUTES / **COOK TIME:** 15 MINUTES
SERVES 4

Crispy kale is a fun topping for a bowl of ramen. It adds both color and textural contrast, plus it's so good for you! And the flavor combination of earthy greens and smoky bacon is divine.

FOR THE KALE
12 leaves Tuscan kale, stemmed and cut into 1-inch pieces
1½ tablespoons olive oil
¼ teaspoon kosher salt
Freshly ground black pepper

FOR THE SOUP
8 cups Basic Pork Broth (page 10) or store-bought broth
½ cup Basic Shoyu Tare (page 18)
18 ounces fresh ramen noodles, 12 ounces dried ramen noodles, or 2 packages instant ramen noodles, cooked according to package directions

2 Soft-Boiled Eggs (page 27), halved
4 strips bacon, cooked until crisp

TO ROAST THE KALE

1. Preheat the oven to 400°F and line a baking sheet with aluminum foil.

2. In a mixing bowl, toss the kale with the olive oil. Spread the kale out on the prepared baking sheet in a single layer, sprinkle the salt and a bit of pepper over it, and roast in the oven for 10 to 15 minutes, until crispy.

TO MAKE THE SOUP

3. In a pot, heat the broth over medium-high heat until simmering.

4. Into each of 4 serving bowls, put 2 tablespoons of tare. Divide the noodles among the bowls and ladle the broth over the noodles. Divide the kale among the bowls and place half an egg and 1 strip of bacon on top of each bowl. Serve immediately.

COOKING TIP: You can make the kale ahead of time and store it in an airtight container for up to 5 days. I like to make a double batch so I have extra for snacking.

PORK RAMEN WITH KIMCHI, FRIED EGGS, AND SPAM

30 MINUTES OR LESS, DAIRY-FREE
PREP TIME: 10 MINUTES / **COOK TIME:** 10 MINUTES
SERVES 4

This Spam-and-eggs ramen is my favorite spin on breakfast for dinner. The kimchi (Korean fermented cabbage) gives it a hit of spice and a nice bit of crunch. You can find kimchi in most Asian markets and many supermarkets.

---

4 (½-inch-thick)
  slices of Spam
4 large eggs
8 cups Basic Pork
  Broth (page 10) **or**
  store-bought broth
½ cup Basic Shoyu Tare
  (page 18)

18 ounces fresh ramen
  noodles, 12 ounces
  dried ramen noodles,
  or 2 packages instant
  ramen noodles,
  cooked according to
  package directions
½ cup kimchi

1. Heat a medium skillet over high heat. Put in the Spam and cook for 3 minutes, until browned on the bottom. Flip over and cook for 3 minutes more, until the second side is browned. Transfer the Spam to a plate.

2. In the same skillet, fry the eggs over medium heat, sunny-side up, until the whites are fully set and the yolks are still a bit runny, about 5 minutes.

3. In a pot, heat the broth over medium-high heat until simmering.

4. Into each of 4 serving bowls, put 2 tablespoons of tare. Divide the noodles among the bowls and ladle the broth over the noodles. Top each bowl with 1 slice of spam and 1 egg. Divide the kimchi among the bowls. Serve immediately.

SUBSTITUTION TIP: If you don't have kimchi, you can substitute 1 cup of finely shredded cabbage and a drizzle of hot chili oil.

Shiso Ramen with
Buttery Clams,
page 90

CHAPTER SIX

SEAFOOD RAMEN

Japan is surrounded by water, so it is no surprise that Japanese cuisine is seafood-rich (hello sushi and sashimi!). Seafood is also used to flavor different varieties of seafood-based ramen. Whether you use fish such as halibut, cod, or salmon or shellfish such as shrimp, clams, or scallops, a bowl of ramen is the perfect way to showcase these delicious treasures of the deep sea.

I love using seafood in ramen because it is a light counterpoint to the starchy noodles. also love the different textures and flavors seafood imparts to a bowl of ramen—from crunchy tempura-fried shrimp, to succulent broiled cod or squid, to clams with a toothsome bite.

CRISPY SHRIMP RAMEN WITH MISO BROTH

30 MINUTES OR LESS, DAIRY-FREE, NUT-FREE OPTION
PREP TIME: 15 MINUTES / **COOK TIME:** 10 MINUTES
SERVES 4

Shrimp tempura is super crispy with a light coating. It is quick and easy to fry on the stovetop. To make this ramen even easier to make, you can buy frozen shrimp tempura and cook it in the oven until browned and crisp. You'll find frozen shrimp tempura in the freezer section of many supermarkets and in Asian markets.

FOR THE SHRIMP
Cooking oil, for frying
⅓ cup ice water
1 large egg
1 cup all-purpose flour
12 large shrimp, peeled and deveined (tails on)
2 tablespoons potato starch or cornstarch
Salt

FOR THE SOUP
2 teaspoons sesame oil
8 ounces kale leaves, center stems removed and leaves cut into ribbons
8 cups Basic Fish Broth (page 12)
½ cup Basic Miso Tare (page 19)

18 ounces fresh ramen noodles, 12 ounces dried ramen noodles, or 2 packages instant ramen noodles, cooked according to package directions

TO MAKE THE SHRIMP

1. Fill a deep-sided pot with about 3 inches of cooking oil and set it over medium-high heat.

2. In a glass measuring cup, whisk together the ice water and egg until well combined.

3. In a medium bowl, combine the flour with the egg and water mixture. Whisk until just combined. Put the potato starch in a shallow bowl.

4. Season the prawns lightly with salt, dredge them in the potato starch, and dunk them in the flour and egg mixture.

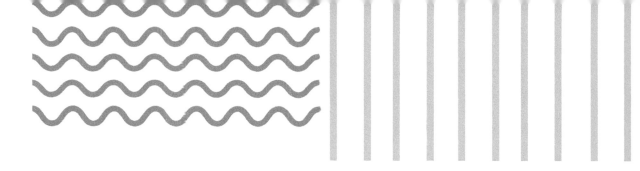

5. Immediately lower the shrimp into the hot oil. Cook for 2 to 3 minutes, until they are golden brown all over. Transfer the cooked shrimp to a paper towel–lined plate to drain.

TO MAKE THE SOUP

6. In a medium skillet, heat the sesame oil over medium-high heat. Add the kale and cook for 3 to 5 minutes, stirring, until tender.

7. In a large pot, heat the broth over medium-high heat until simmering.

8. Into each of 4 serving bowls, put 2 tablespoons of tare. Divide the noodles among the bowls and ladle the broth over the noodles. Divide the prawns and kale among the bowls. Serve immediately.

COOKING TIP: Use a deep-sided, heavy-bottomed saucepan or small Dutch oven for deep frying. The high sides will contain oil spatters, making cleanup easier.

GINGER-MISO SALMON RAMEN WITH BROCCOLI

DAIRY-FREE, NUT-FREE OPTION

PREP TIME: 15 MINUTES, PLUS 15 MINUTES TO CHILL / **COOK TIME:** 15 MINUTES

SERVES 4

This salmon, with its savory-sweet glaze, is a favorite in my house, whether I serve it over ramen or over a bowl of steamed rice. It's quick and easy to make and uses only a handful of pantry ingredients. Broccoli adds a green element and gives you your requisite serving of healthy vegetables.

FOR THE SALMON

- 3 tablespoons miso (preferably white miso or a combination of white and red)
- 2 tablespoons sake
- 2 tablespoons sugar
- 2 tablespoons soy sauce
- 2 teaspoons peeled, minced fresh ginger
- 4 (4- to 6-ounce) salmon fillets

FOR THE SOUP

- 1 small broccoli head, cut into florets
- ⅓ cup water
- 8 cups Basic Fish Broth (page 12)
- ½ cup Basic Miso Tare (page 19)

- 18 ounces fresh ramen noodles, 12 ounces dried ramen noodles, or 2 packages instant ramen noodles, cooked according to package directions
- 4 teaspoons Scallion Oil (page 29)
- 2 tablespoons toasted sesame seeds

TO MAKE THE SALMON

1. Preheat the oven to 425°F and line a baking sheet with aluminum foil or parchment paper.

2. In a small bowl, stir together the miso, sake, sugar, soy sauce, and ginger until the mixture is smooth.

3. Arrange the salmon fillets on the prepared baking sheet and spoon the miso mixture over them. Refrigerate the salmon for about 15 minutes.

4. Roast the salmon for about 10 minutes, until the fish is cooked through and flakes easily with a fork.

TO MAKE THE SOUP

5. While the salmon is cooking, place the broccoli in a microwave-safe bowl and add the water. Cover the bowl with a plate or plastic wrap and heat in the microwave on high for 4 to 5 minutes, until the broccoli is tender. Remove the bowl and uncover it. Drain.

6. In a pot, heat the broth over medium-high heat until simmering.

7. Into each of 4 serving bowls, put 2 tablespoons of tare. Divide the noodles among the bowls and ladle the broth over the noodles. Arrange 1 salmon fillet and several broccoli florets on top of each bowl. Garnish with the scallion oil and sesame seeds and serve immediately.

SUBSTITUTION TIP: If you don't have scallion oil, substitute 4 thinly sliced scallions.

MISO BLACK COD RAMEN

DAIRY-FREE, NUT-FREE

PREP TIME: 15 MINUTES, PLUS 24 HOURS TO MARINATE / **COOK TIME:** 25 MINUTES

SERVES 4

These black cod fillets are seasoned with miso paste and marinated for a full 24 hours (or more) for maximum flavor absorption. The fish is baked until the skin blackens and the flesh is succulent and flaky. If you have the time, you'll find this dish is well worth the wait. Black cod is a delicate but flavorful white fish, which is also called sablefish or butterfish. If you can't find it, you can substitute Chilean sea bass.

FOR THE FISH

4 (4- to 6-ounce) black cod fillets, with skin

Kosher salt

¼ cup plus 2 tablespoons white miso paste

¼ cup mirin

2 tablespoons sake

FOR THE SOUP

8 cups Basic Fish Broth (page 12)

½ cup Basic Shoyu Tare (page 18)

18 ounces fresh ramen noodles, 12 ounces dried ramen noodles, or 2 packages instant ramen noodles, cooked according to package directions

2 cups arugula

2 to 4 teaspoons chili oil

TO MAKE THE FISH

1. Season the fillets generously with salt and let them stand for 15 to 20 minutes. Use a paper towel to wipe the salt off the fish and pat it dry.

2. In a small bowl, stir together the miso, mirin, and sake until smooth.

3. Place the fish in a baking dish large enough to fit all the fillets in a single layer. Pour the miso mixture over the top. Turn the fish pieces over to coat them completely with the marinade. Cover and refrigerate for at least 24 hours or as long as 3 days.

4. Preheat the oven to 400°F and line a rimmed baking sheet with aluminum foil or parchment paper.

5. Remove the fillets from the marinade and wipe any excess marinade off with your fingers. Arrange the fish in a single layer with the skin side up on the prepared baking sheet. Bake for 20 to 25 minutes, until the skin is blackened and the fish flakes easily with a fork.

TO MAKE THE SOUP

6. In a pot, heat the broth over medium-high heat until simmering.

7. Into each of 4 serving bowls, put 2 tablespoons of tare. Divide the noodles among the bowls and ladle the broth over the noodles. Arrange 1 fish fillet on each bowl and divide the arugula among the bowls. Drizzle ½ to 1 teaspoon of chili oil over each bowl and serve immediately.

COOKING TIP: The longer you marinate the fish, the more the flavors will permeate. You can marinate it for up to 3 days in the refrigerator. You can also freeze it for up to 3 weeks. Thaw the fish overnight in the refrigerator before cooking.

SHOYU RAMEN WITH PANFRIED SHRIMP AND GREENS

30 MINUTES OR LESS, DAIRY-FREE, NUT-FREE
PREP TIME: 10 MINUTES / **COOK TIME:** 10 MINUTES
SERVES 4

A quick shrimp and greens stir-fry makes a perfect topping for this simple bowl of ramen using a basic fish broth. If you like a spicy kick to your ramen, add a drizzle of Sesame-Chili Oil (page 30), store-bought chili oil, or a sprinkle of Shichimi Togarashi (page 31).

FOR THE SHRIMP AND GREENS
½ cup soy sauce
2 tablespoons honey
1 tablespoon sesame oil
1 tablespoon cornstarch
1 tablespoon water
4 garlic cloves, minced
1 teaspoon chili paste
1 tablespoon cooking oil
1½ pounds shrimp, peeled and deveined

10 leaves chard or kale, tough center ribs removed and leaves julienned

FOR THE SOUP
8 cups Basic Fish Broth (page 12)
½ cup Basic Shoyu Tare (page 18)

18 ounces fresh ramen noodles, 12 ounces dried ramen noodles, or 2 packages instant ramen noodles, cooked according to package directions
4 scallions, both white and green parts, thinly sliced
4 teaspoons toasted sesame seeds

TO MAKE THE SHRIMP AND GREENS

1. In a small bowl, whisk together the soy sauce, honey, sesame oil, cornstarch, water, garlic, and chili paste.

2. In a large skillet, heat the oil over medium-high heat. Add the shrimp and cook for about 3 minutes, stirring, until it is opaque and just cooked through.

3. Add the greens to the pan and cook, stirring, until the greens are wilted, about 3 minutes more.

4. Add the sauce mixture to the skillet and cook for about 2 minutes, until it bubbles and thickens.

TO MAKE THE SOUP

5. In a pot, heat the broth over medium-high heat until simmering.

6. Into each of 4 serving bowls, put 2 tablespoons of tare. Divide the noodles among the bowls and ladle the broth over the noodles. Divide the shrimp and greens among the bowls. Garnish with the scallions and sesame seeds and serve immediately.

INGREDIENT TIP: Buy your shrimp peeled and deveined to save time on prep.

SHOYU RAMEN WITH LEMONY BREADED HALIBUT

30 MINUTES OR LESS, DAIRY-FREE, NUT-FREE
PREP TIME: 15 MINUTES / **COOK TIME:** 15 MINUTES
SERVES 4

Crispy halibut fillets make a nice textural contrast for a bowl of noodles in broth. Here the crust is scented with lemon zest, giving it a fresh punch. Encourage diners to squeeze lemon juice into their bowls and over the fish just before eating.

FOR THE FISH
2 tablespoons mayonnaise
4 (5-ounce) halibut fillets
¾ cup panko bread crumbs
Zest of 1 lemon
Kosher salt
Freshly ground pepper

FOR THE SOUP
8 cups Basic Fish Broth (page 12)
½ cup Basic Shoyu Tare (page 18)
18 ounces fresh ramen noodles, 12 ounces dried ramen noodles, or 2 packages instant ramen noodles, cooked according to package directions

2 Soy Sauce Eggs (page 28), halved
2 cups arugula
4 scallions, both white and green parts, thinly sliced
4 lemon wedges

TO MAKE THE FISH

1. Preheat the oven to 400°F. Line a rimmed baking sheet with aluminum foil.

2. Spread the mayonnaise on the fish fillets in a thin layer, completely coating each fillet.

3. In a shallow bowl, toss together the panko and lemon zest, and season the mixture with salt and pepper.

4. Press each fillet into the bread crumb mixture to coat completely. Arrange the coated fillets on the prepared baking sheet.

5. Bake for 15 minutes, or until the fish is cooked through and flakes easily with a fork.

TO MAKE THE SOUP

6. In a pot, heat the broth over medium-high heat until simmering.

7. Into each of 4 serving bowls, put 2 tablespoons of tare. Divide the noodles among the bowls and ladle the broth over the noodles. In each bowl, arrange 1 fish fillet and half an egg on top and divide the arugula among the bowls. Garnish with the scallions and a lemon wedge and serve immediately.

SUBSTITUTION TIP: You can use any mild white fish in place of halibut; cod or pollock both work well.

SHOYU SHRIMP TEMPURA RAMEN

30 MINUTES OR LESS, DAIRY-FREE, NUT-FREE
PREP TIME: 15 MINUTES / **COOK TIME:** 5 MINUTES
SERVES 4

There are few things I love as much as a bowl of ramen, but shrimp tempura is one of them. The plump shrimp are coated in a shatteringly crisp fried-batter shell, making them the perfect counterpoint to a bowl of broth and noodles.

FOR THE SHRIMP
Cooking oil, for frying
1 pound large shrimp
   (about 12 shrimp),
   peeled and deveined
½ cup cornstarch
1 cup all-purpose flour
½ teaspoon kosher salt
1 large egg
¼ cup club soda

FOR THE SOUP
8 cups Basic Fish Broth
   (page 12)
½ cup Basic Shoyu Tare
   (page 18)
18 ounces fresh ramen
   noodles, 12 ounces
   dried ramen noodles,
   or 2 packages instant
   ramen noodles,
   cooked according to
   package directions

2 Soy Sauce Eggs
   (page 28) or
   Soft-Boiled Eggs
   (page 27), halved
4 scallions, both white
   and green parts,
   thinly sliced

TO MAKE THE SHRIMP

1. Fill a deep-sided saucepan with 2 to 3 inches of oil. Heat it over medium-high heat until it shimmers.

2. In a bowl, toss the shrimp in the cornstarch to coat.

3. In a medium bowl, whisk together the flour and salt. In small bowl, whisk together the egg and club soda until frothy. Whisk the egg mixture into the flour mixture until smooth.

4. Dunk the shrimp in the batter to coat and drop them into the hot oil. Cook for about 3 minutes, until golden brown. Transfer the shrimp to a paper towel–lined plate to drain.

TO MAKE THE SOUP

5. In a pot, heat the broth over medium-high heat until simmering.

6. Into each of 4 serving bowls, put 2 tablespoons of tare. Divide the noodles among the bowls and ladle the broth over the noodles. Divide the shrimp and eggs among the bowls. Garnish each bowl with scallions and serve immediately.

SUBSTITUTION TIP: I wholeheartedly support substituting store-bought frozen shrimp tempura here. Just be sure to cook them until they are nicely browned and very crisp.

SHIO RAMEN WITH BUTTERY CLAMS

30 MINUTES OR LESS, DAIRY-FREE, GLUTEN-FREE (USE GLUTEN-FREE NOODLES), NUT-FREE

PREP TIME: 10 MINUTES / **COOK TIME:** 10 MINUTES

SERVES 4

Shellfish is a quick-cooking ramen topping. Live clams may seem a bit intimidating, but they are very easy to cook and look really cool on top of a bowl of ramen. Here a bit of butter melts right on top of each clam, giving it rich flavor.

---

1 pound live littleneck clams, cleaned

8 cups Basic Fish Broth (page 12)

½ cup Basic Shio Tare (page 17)

18 ounces fresh ramen noodles, 12 ounces dried ramen noodles, or 2 packages instant ramen noodles, cooked according to package directions

¼ cup (½ stick) butter, cut into small pieces

4 scallions, both white and green parts, thinly sliced

1. Fill a medium saucepan with about 4 inches of water and bring it to a boil over high heat.

2. Add the clams, reduce the heat to medium, cover, and cook for about 10 minutes. The clam shells will open as they cook. Using a slotted spoon, remove the clams carefully from the water. Discard any clams that do not open.

3. In a pot, heat the broth over medium-high heat until simmering.

4. Into each of 4 serving bowls, put 2 tablespoons of tare. Divide the noodles among the bowls and ladle the broth over the noodles. Arrange several clams on top of each bowl and top each clam with a bit of butter. Garnish with the scallions and serve immediately.

SUBSTITUTION TIP: You can substitute frozen clams in their shells for the live clams. Thaw them in the refrigerator overnight and then cook as directed.

RAMEN WITH SAUTÉED SQUID AND ARUGULA

30 MINUTES OR LESS, DAIRY-FREE, NUT-FREE

PREP TIME: 10 MINUTES, PLUS 10 MINUTES TO MARINATE / **COOK TIME:** 5 MINUTES

SERVES 4

Squid is easy to cook and inexpensive, making it a perfect way to top a bowl of ramen. Here it is marinated in soy sauce, mirin, and ginger, and then stir-fried for just a few minutes. I love the combination of the gingery sautéed squid with peppery arugula.

FOR THE SQUID

1 pound squid, bodies
    thinly sliced

3 tablespoons soy sauce

2 tablespoons peeled,
    minced fresh ginger

2 tablespoons mirin

2 tablespoons cooking oil

FOR THE SOUP

8 cups Basic Fish Broth
    (page 12)

½ cup Basic Shoyu Tare
    (page 18)

18 ounces fresh ramen
    noodles, 12 ounces
    dried ramen noodles,
    or 2 packages instant
    ramen noodles,
    cooked according to
    package directions

2 Soft-Boiled Eggs
    (page 27), **halved**

2 cups arugula

TO MAKE THE SQUID

1. In a medium bowl, combine the squid, soy sauce, ginger, and mirin, and toss well. Let the squid stand for 10 to 15 minutes.

2. In a large skillet, heat the oil over medium-high heat.

3. Using a slotted spoon, lift the squid out of the bowl, leaving the marinade behind in the bowl, and add it to the pan. Cook for 5 minutes, stirring, until the squid is just cooked through.

CONTINUED

TO MAKE THE SOUP

4. In a pot, heat the broth over medium-high heat until simmering.

5. Into each of 4 serving bowls, put 2 tablespoons of tare. Divide the noodles among the bowls and ladle the broth over the noodles. Divide the squid, eggs, and arugula among the bowls. Serve immediately.

INGREDIENT TIP: Squid is super easy to cook but can be a hassle to clean. If you can, buy your squid already cleaned to save time.

SALT-BROILED SALMON RAMEN WITH CORN AND GREENS

30 MINUTES OR LESS DAIRY-FREE, NUT-FREE
PREP TIME: 10 MINUTES / **COOK TIME:** 20 MINUTES
SERVES 4

Salt broiling or grilling (shioyaki) is a common Japanese technique for preparing fish, especially fatty fishes like salmon or mackerel. I especially love to use this method to cook salmon because it makes it especially flaky and flavorful. This salmon is a great, easy topping for a bowl of ramen.

FOR THE SALMON
4 (4- to 6-ounce) salmon fillets, patted dry
1 teaspoon kosher salt
1 tablespoon cooking oil
10 chard or kale leaves, tough center ribs removed, leaves julienned
1½ cups fresh or frozen corn kernels

FOR THE SOUP
8 cups Basic Fish Broth (page 12)
½ cup Basic Shoyu Tare (page 18)
18 ounces fresh ramen noodles, 12 ounces dried ramen noodles, or 2 packages instant ramen noodles, cooked according to package directions

4 teaspoons Sesame-Chili Oil (page 30) **or store-bought sesame oil or chili oil**

TO MAKE THE SALMON

1. Preheat the broiler to high.

2. Season the salmon fillets on both sides with the salt and put them on a baking sheet.

3. Broil the salmon for 8 minutes, until it is cooked through and flakes easily with a fork.

4. In a medium skillet, heat the oil over medium-high heat. Add the greens and cook for 4 minutes, stirring, until wilted. Transfer them to a bowl.

CONTINUED

5. Add the corn to the skillet and cook for 3 minutes, stirring, just until heated through and beginning to brown.

TO MAKE THE SOUP

6. In a pot, heat the broth over medium-high heat until simmering.

7. Into each of 4 serving bowls, put 2 tablespoons of tare. Divide the noodles among the bowls and ladle the broth over the noodles. Top each bowl with a salmon fillet and divide the greens among the bowls. Drizzle each bowl with 1 teaspoon of sesame-chili oil. Serve immediately.

COOKING TIP: Salt the salmon fillets and then refrigerate them, covered, overnight. This will make their texture even more meaty and the fish even more flavorful.

Shio Ramen with
Teriyaki Beef and
Broccoli, *page 110*

CHAPTER SEVEN

BEEF RAMEN

In Japan, most ramen broths and toppings use pork and chicken, but a rich, meaty ramen using beef broth and/or topped with beef is delicious as well. For any of these ramens, you can substitute pork or chicken broth if you prefer.

The recipes in this chapter use various cuts of beef (flank steak, short ribs, thinly sliced sirloin, ground beef, and more) and different cooking methods. You'll find everything from juicy grilled steak to flavorful meatballs made from ground beef. Potatoes, bok choy, sautéed chard, and daikon radish are among the vegetables that play supporting roles in these meat-centric bowls.

MISO RAMEN WITH GINGER MEATBALLS

DAIRY-FREE, NUT-FREE OPTION
PREP TIME: 15 MINUTES / **COOK TIME:** 20 MINUTES
SERVES 4

Ginger meatballs are a great way to use ground beef in a ramen-friendly way. Fresh ginger, garlic, scallions, and soy sauce flavor these meaty morsels. Baking them on a sheet pan in the oven is a convenient way to cook them all at once and can be done while you prep the other elements of the soup.

FOR THE MEATBALLS

1 pound ground beef
½ cup panko
   bread crumbs
1 large egg
3 scallions, both white
   and green parts,
   thinly sliced
1 tablespoon peeled,
   minced fresh ginger
1 tablespoon soy sauce
2 teaspoons sesame oil
2 garlic cloves, minced
2 tablespoons cooking oil

FOR THE SOUP

8 cups Basic Beef
   Broth (page 11) or
   store-bought broth
8 to 12 baby bok choy
½ cup Basic Miso Tare
   (page 19)

18 ounces fresh ramen
   noodles, 12 ounces
   dried ramen noodles,
   or 2 packages instant
   ramen noodles,
   cooked according to
   package directions
½ cup sliced
   bamboo shoots

TO MAKE THE MEATBALLS

1. Preheat the oven to 450°F and line a rimmed baking sheet with aluminum foil.

2. In a medium bowl, combine the ground beef, panko, egg, scallions, ginger, soy sauce, sesame oil, and garlic, and mix well. Form the mixture into 1½-inch balls and arrange them on the prepared baking sheet.

3. Brush the tops of the meatballs with oil and bake for about 15 minutes, until they are cooked through and browned.

TO MAKE THE SOUP

4. In a pot, heat the broth over medium-high heat until simmering. Add the bok choy and cook for 3 to 4 minutes, until wilted.

5. Into each of 4 serving bowls, put 2 tablespoons of tare. Divide the noodles among the bowls and ladle the broth over the noodles. Divide the meatballs, baby bok choy, and bamboo shoots, and arrange them on top of each bowl. Serve immediately.

COOKING TIP: Use a small cookie scoop to form the meatballs. It will save time and give you uniformly sized meatballs.

MISO RAMEN WITH BRAISED BEEF AND POTATOES

DAIRY-FREE, NUT-FREE OPTION

PREP TIME: 15 MINUTES / **COOK TIME:** 1 HOUR 15 MINUTES

SERVES 4

This is a meat-and-potatoes lover's ramen. Tender chunks of beef are braised in a mixture of soy sauce, ginger, and mirin. The thick stew makes a hearty topping for a bowl of ramen. A sprinkle of fresh parsley adds color and freshness.

FOR THE BEEF

1 tablespoon cooking oil

1 pound beef stew meat, cut into 1½-inch pieces

1 cup Basic Chicken Broth (page 9), **Basic Beef Broth** (page 11), **or** store-bought broth

2 tablespoons soy sauce

2 tablespoons mirin

1½-inch piece fresh ginger, peeled and sliced

1 pound potatoes, peeled and cut into chunks

FOR THE SOUP

8 cups Basic Beef Broth (page 11) **or** store-bought broth

½ cup Basic Miso Tare (page 19)

18 ounces fresh ramen noodles, 12 ounces dried ramen noodles, or 2 packages instant ramen noodles, cooked according to package directions

¼ cup chopped fresh parsley

TO MAKE THE BEEF

1. In a Dutch oven or heavy-bottomed saucepan, heat the oil over medium-high heat. Add the meat and cook for 8 minutes, stirring every couple of minutes, until nicely browned all over.

2. Add the broth and cook over high heat for about 3 minutes, scraping up the browned bits from the bottom of the pan. Add the soy sauce, mirin, and ginger.

3. Reduce the heat to medium-low, cover the pot, and cook for about 45 minutes, until the meat is tender.

4. Add the potatoes, cover again, and cook for 15 to 20 minutes, until the potatoes are tender.

TO MAKE THE SOUP

5. In a pot, heat the broth over medium-high heat until simmering.

6. Into each of 4 serving bowls, put 2 tablespoons of tare. Divide the noodles among the bowls and ladle the broth over the noodles. Divide the meat and potatoes among the bowls. Garnish with the parsley and serve immediately.

VARIATION TIP: Substitute daikon radish for the potatoes for a slightly different flavor. When cooked, daikon has a similar texture to potatoes and a nice radish-y bite.

SPICY MISO RAMEN WITH SAUTÉED SLICED BEEF

30 MINUTES OR LESS, DAIRY-FREE, NUT-FREE OPTION
PREP TIME: 10 MINUTES / **COOK TIME:** 10 MINUTES
SERVES 4

This is a quick version of braised beef using thinly sliced sirloin, which doesn't need to cook as long as stew meat, making this a quick weeknight ramen. The spicy miso pairs well with the beef to create a warming bowl loaded with umami.

FOR THE BEEF
½ cup Basic Beef Broth (page 11), **store-bought broth, or water**
2 tablespoons soy sauce
2 tablespoons mirin
1 tablespoon sake
1 tablespoon sugar
½ onion, thinly sliced
12 ounces thinly sliced beef, such top sirloin

FOR THE SOUP
8 cups Basic Beef Broth (page 11) **or store-bought broth**
½ cup Spicy Miso Tare (page 19)
18 ounces fresh ramen noodles, 12 ounces dried ramen noodles, or 2 packages instant ramen noodles, cooked according to package directions

1 cup Marinated Bean Sprouts (page 23) **or fresh bean sprouts**
4 scallions, both white and green parts, thinly sliced
4 teaspoons sesame oil

TO MAKE THE BEEF

1. In a large skillet, combine the broth, soy sauce, mirin, sake, and sugar, and bring the mixture to a boil. Add the onion, cover the skillet, and cook for about 5 minutes, until the onion is tender.

2. Add the beef to the skillet and cook, uncovered, until the meat is just cooked through, 5 minutes more.

TO MAKE THE SOUP

3. In a pot, heat the broth over medium-high heat until simmering.

4. Into each of 4 serving bowls, put 2 tablespoons of tare. Divide the noodles among the bowls and ladle the broth over the noodles. Divide the meat and bean sprouts among the bowls. Garnish with the scallions and sesame oil and serve immediately.

VARIATION TIP: The beef on its own is delicious served over steamed rice.

MISO RAMEN WITH STIR-FRIED SESAME GROUND BEEF

30 MINUTES OR LESS, DAIRY-FREE, NUT-FREE OPTION
PREP TIME: 10 MINUTES / **COOK TIME:** 10 MINUTES
SERVES 4

The stir-fried ground beef that tops this bowl of ramen is super flavorful, especially when paired with fresh grated carrots and thinly sliced snap peas. The drizzle of sesame-chili oil or plain chili oil really pulls the dish together and takes it to the next level. If you don't like too much spice, substitute sesame oil instead.

FOR THE BEEF
1 pound ground beef
3 garlic cloves, minced
1 tablespoon peeled, minced fresh ginger
⅓ cup soy sauce
⅓ cup packed brown sugar
1 tablespoon sesame oil

FOR THE SOUP
8 cups Basic Beef Broth (page 11) or store-bought broth
½ cup Spicy Miso Tare (page 19)
18 ounces fresh ramen noodles, 12 ounces dried ramen noodles, or 2 packages instant ramen noodles, cooked according to package directions
½ cup sugar snap peas, sliced
½ cup shredded carrots
4 scallions, both white and green parts, thinly sliced
4 teaspoons Sesame-Chili Oil (page 30) or store-bought chili oil

TO MAKE THE BEEF

1. Heat a large skillet over medium-high heat. Put in the beef and cook for 5 minutes, stirring and breaking it up with a spatula, until browned. Transfer the meat to a bowl and discard any excess grease left in the skillet.

2. Add the garlic and ginger to the skillet and cook, stirring, for about 30 seconds. Return the beef to the skillet.

3. In a small bowl, stir together the soy sauce, brown sugar, and sesame oil. Pour the mixture over the meat and simmer for about 2 minutes more, until the flavors meld.

TO MAKE THE SOUP

4. In a pot, heat the broth over medium-high heat until simmering.

5. Into each of 4 serving bowls, put 2 tablespoons of tare. Divide the noodles among the bowls and ladle the broth over the noodles. Divide the meat, snap peas, carrots, and scallions, and arrange them in the bowls. Drizzle the sesame-chili oil over the top and serve immediately.

SUBSTITUTION TIP: You can substitute any ground meat for the beef; pork, chicken, or turkey will all work well.

SHIO RAMEN WITH 5-SPICE BEEF SHORT RIBS

DAIRY-FREE, NUT-FREE

PREP TIME: 10 MINUTES / **COOK TIME:** 4 HOURS 10 MINUTES

SERVES 4

Beef short ribs braised in broth scented with Chinese five-spice powder are easy to make and sure to impress. Chinese five-spice powder includes cinnamon, cloves, fennel, star anise, and Szechuan peppercorns and is available in the spice section of most super-markets. Cooking the ribs takes a while but results in meltingly tender meat that makes a delightful topping for a bowl of ramen.

FOR THE SHORT RIBS

¼ cup sugar

3 tablespoons rice vinegar

3 cups Basic Beef Broth (page 11) **or** store-bought broth

¼ cup soy sauce

2 pounds bone-in short ribs, cut into 2-inch pieces

5 garlic cloves, peeled

3 scallions, both white and green parts, halved lengthwise

2-inch piece fresh ginger, peeled and thinly sliced

1 teaspoon Chinese five-spice powder

FOR THE SOUP

8 cups Basic Beef Broth (page 11) **or** store-bought broth

½ cup Basic Shio Tare (page 17)

18 ounces fresh ramen noodles, 12 ounces dried ramen noodles, or 2 packages instant ramen noodles, cooked according to package directions

1 cup radish sprouts or mung bean sprouts

4 teaspoons Sesame-Chili Oil (page 30) **or** store-bought chili oil

TO MAKE THE SHORT RIBS

1. In a large saucepan or Dutch oven, heat the sugar and vinegar over medium-high heat for 5 minutes, stirring, until the sugar dissolves and the mixture becomes syrupy. Stir in the broth and soy sauce.

2. Add the ribs, garlic, scallions, ginger, and five-spice powder. Reduce the heat to low, cover the pot, and simmer for about 4 hours, until the meat is very tender.

TO MAKE THE SOUP

3. In a pot, heat the broth over medium-high heat until simmering.

4. Into each of 4 serving bowls, put 2 tablespoons of tare. Divide the noodles among the bowls and ladle the broth over the noodles. Divide the meat and sprouts among the bowls. Drizzle the sesame-chili oil over the top and serve immediately.

INGREDIENT TIP: Ask your butcher to cut the ribs into 2-inch pieces for you.

SHIO RAMEN WITH CURRIED BEEF WITH PEAS AND CARROTS

30 MINUTES OR LESS, DAIRY-FREE, NUT-FREE
PREP TIME: 10 MINUTES / **COOK TIME:** 15 MINUTES
SERVES 4

Curry is so popular in Japan that it is considered one of the country's national dishes. Japanese curry is sweeter and milder than Indian or Thai curries, but it is still full of flavor. It is served both over rice and as a topping for ramen. This curry is typical, even down to the packaged curry seasoning that Japanese cooks swear by.

FOR THE BEEF

2 tablespoons cooking oil

1 pound top sirloin, thinly sliced

4 cups Basic Chicken Broth (page 9), **Basic Beef Broth** (page 11), **or store-bought broth**

1 (8-ounce) package Japanese curry mix

2 carrots, peeled and diced

1 cup frozen peas

FOR THE SOUP

8 cups Basic Beef Broth (page 11) **or store-bought broth**

½ cup Basic Shio Tare (page 17)

18 ounces fresh ramen noodles, 12 ounces dried ramen noodles, or 2 packages instant ramen noodles, cooked according to package directions

2 Soft-Boiled Eggs (page 27), **halved**

4 scallions, both white and green parts, thinly sliced

TO MAKE THE BEEF

1. In a large skillet, heat the oil over medium-high heat. Add the beef and cook, stirring, until just cooked through, 5 minutes. Stir in the broth and curry. Add the carrots and bring to a boil. Reduce the heat to medium-low and simmer until the carrots are tender, about 5 minutes. Stir in the peas and cook just until heated through, 2 minutes more.

TO MAKE THE SOUP

2. In a pot, heat the broth over medium-high heat until simmering.

3. Into each of 4 serving bowls, place 2 tablespoons of the tare. Divide the noodles among the bowls and ladle the broth over the noodles. Divide the meat and sauce, veggies, eggs, and scallions among the bowls. Serve immediately.

STORAGE TIP: The beef curry can be made ahead of time and stored in the refrigerator for up to 3 days.

SHIO RAMEN WITH TERIYAKI BEEF AND BROCCOLI

30 MINUTES, DAIRY-FREE, NUT-FREE
PREP TIME: 10 MINUTES / **COOK TIME:** 10 MINUTES
SERVES 4

Using thinly sliced beef and store-bought teriyaki sauce, this recipe comes together in a flash. Sweet and savory teriyaki beef is always a crowd pleaser, and putting it on top of ramen only makes it more appealing.

FOR THE BEEF AND BROCCOLI

¼ cup water

¼ cup teriyaki sauce

2 teaspoons cornstarch

1 teaspoon sugar

1 teaspoon sesame oil

3 tablespoons cooking oil, divided

1 pound flank steak, thinly sliced

1 small head broccoli, cut into florets

1 tablespoon peeled, minced fresh ginger

2 garlic cloves, minced

FOR THE SOUP

8 cups Basic Beef Broth (page 11) or store-bought broth

½ cup Basic Shio Tare (page 17)

18 ounces fresh ramen noodles, 12 ounces dried ramen noodles, or 2 packages instant ramen noodles, cooked according to package directions

4 scallions, both white and green parts, thinly sliced

2 tablespoons toasted sesame seeds

TO MAKE THE BEEF AND BROCCOLI

1. In a small bowl, stir together the water, teriyaki sauce, cornstarch, sugar, and sesame oil.

2. In a large skillet, heat 2 tablespoons of oil over high heat. Cook the beef for 3 minutes, stirring, until it is browned all over and just cooked through. Transfer the beef to a bowl or plate.

3. In the same skil et, heat the remaining 1 tablespoon of oil and add the broccoli. Cook, stirring often, for about 2 minutes, until the broccoli begins to soften. Lower the heat to medium and stir in the ginger and garlic. Add the sauce mixture and bring to a boil. Cook until the sauce thickens, 1 minute. Return the beef to the skillet and stir to coat well. Remove the pan from the heat.

TO MAKE THE SOUP

4. In a pot, heat the broth over medium-high heat until simmering.

5. Into each of 4 serving bowls, put 2 tablespoons of tare. Divide the noodles among the bowls and ladle the broth over the noodles. Divide the beef, broccoli, and scallions among the bowls. Garnish with the sesame seeds and serve immediately.

COOKING TIP: To make the beef easier to cut into thin slices, pop it in the freezer for about 30 minutes first.

SHIO RAMEN WITH HOISIN BEEF

30 MINUTES OR LESS, DAIRY-FREE
PREP TIME: 10 MINUTES / **COOK TIME:** 15 MINUTES
SERVES 4

The combination of sweet-savory hoisin sauce, creamy peanut butter, and spicy sriracha gives this beef topping irresistible appeal. Sautéed greens, scallions, and soft-boiled eggs round out the bowl nicely.

FOR THE BEEF AND GREENS

1 pound ground beef

2 garlic cloves, minced

1 teaspoon peeled, grated fresh ginger

¼ cup smooth peanut butter

3 tablespoons hoisin sauce

1½ teaspoons sriracha

1 tablespoon soy sauce

1 tablespoon cooking oil

10 chard or kale leaves, tough center ribs removed and leaves julienned

Pinch kosher salt

FOR THE SOUP

8 cups Basic Beef Broth (page 11) **or** store-bought broth

½ cup Basic Shio Tare (page 17)

18 ounces fresh ramen noodles, 12 ounces dried ramen noodles, or 2 packages instant ramen noodles, cooked according to package directions

2 Soft-Boiled Eggs (page 27), **halved**

4 scallions, both white and green parts, thinly sliced

2 tablespoons chopped peanuts

TO MAKE THE BEEF AND GREENS

1. In a skillet, cook the beef for 6 to 8 minutes over medium-high heat, stirring and breaking up the meat with a spatula, until browned. Drain any excess fat from the skillet.

2. Stir the garlic and ginger into the beef and cook for about 30 seconds more. Add the peanut butter, hoisin sauce, and sriracha, and stir to combine. Remove the pan from the heat. Transfer the meat and sauce to a bowl and wipe out the skillet.

3. In the same skillet, heat the oil over medium-high heat. Add the greens and salt and cook for 3 minutes, stirring, until wilted.

TO MAKE THE SOUP

4. In a pot, heat the broth over medium-high heat until simmering.

5. Into each of 4 serving bowls, put 2 tablespoons of tare. Divide the noodles among the bowls and ladle the broth over the noodles. Divide the beef, greens, eggs, and scallions among the bowls. Garnish with the peanuts and serve immediately.

SUBSTITUTION TIP: You can use any leafy greens in place of the kale or chard. Try using mustard greens, which have a bit of a spicy kick.

SHOYU RAMEN WITH GRILLED FLANK STEAK

30 MINUTES OR LESS, DAIRY-FREE, NUT-FREE
PREP TIME: 15 MINUTES / **COOK TIME:** 10 MINUTES
SERVES 4

Flank steak is ideal for grilling and turns out tender and flavorful. Here it adds smokiness to a simple bowl of shoyu ramen. Cook the meat to just medium-rare for the most flavor and, to keep it moist and tender, be sure to let it rest before you slice it.

FOR THE BEEF
1 pound flank steak
1½ teaspoons sesame oil
1 teaspoon kosher salt
½ teaspoon freshly ground black pepper

FOR THE SOUP
8 cups Basic Beef Broth (page 11) or store-bought broth
½ cup Basic Shoyu Tare (page 18)
18 ounces fresh ramen noodles, 12 ounces dried ramen noodles, or 2 packages instant ramen noodles, cooked according to package directions

4 scallions, both white and green parts, thinly sliced
2 tablespoons toasted sesame seeds
Shichimi Togarashi (page 31), for garnish (optional)

TO MAKE THE BEEF

1. Heat a grill or grill pan over medium-high heat.

2. Rub the steak all over with the sesame oil and season it with the salt and pepper.

3. Grill the steak, flipping it one time, until it is cooked to your desired doneness, 6 to 8 minutes for medium-rare.

4. Transfer the steak to a cutting board and let it stand, uncovered, for 5 minutes. Thinly slice the steak across the grain.

TO MAKE THE SOUP

5. In a pot, heat the broth over medium-high heat until simmering.

6. Into each of 4 serving bowls, put 2 tablespoons of tare. Divide the noodles among the bowls and ladle the broth over the noodles. Divide the steak and scallions among the bowls. Garnish with the sesame seeds and a sprinkle of shichimi togarashi (if using). Serve immediately.

SUBSTITUTION TIP: You can substitute skirt steak or flat iron steak for the flank steak.

SHOYU RAMEN WITH GARLICKY GROUND BEEF

30 MINUTES OR LESS, DAIRY-FREE, NUT-FREE
PREP TIME: 10 MINUTES / **COOK TIME:** 15 MINUTES
SERVES 4

This stir-fry is flavored with lots of garlic, a bit of sugar, and some crushed red pepper that makes it addictive. Radish sprouts add a nice fresh element with a little bit of kick.

FOR THE BEEF

1 pound ground beef

4 garlic cloves, minced

1 tablespoon peeled, grated fresh ginger

2 teaspoons sesame oil

¼ cup soy sauce

2 tablespoons brown sugar

¼ teaspoon red pepper flakes

FOR THE SOUP

8 cups Basic Beef Broth (page 11) or store-bought broth

½ cup Basic Shoyu Tare (page 18)

18 ounces fresh ramen noodles, 12 ounces dried ramen noodles, or 2 packages instant ramen noodles, cooked according to package directions

2 Soy Sauce Eggs (page 28), halved

¼ cup radish sprouts

TO MAKE THE BEEF

1. In a large skillet, cook the beef for 5 to 7 minutes over medium-high heat, stirring and breaking up the meat with a spatula, until browned. Drain off any excess grease. Add the garlic, ginger, and sesame oil and cook, stirring, for 2 minutes. Add the soy sauce, brown sugar, and red pepper, and cook for about 5 minutes, stirring occasionally, until the sauce is reduced.

TO MAKE THE SOUP

2. In a pot, heat the broth over medium-high heat until simmering.

3. Into each of 4 serving bowls, put 2 tablespoons of tare. Divide the noodles among the bowls and ladle the broth over the noodles. Divide the beef, eggs, and sprouts among the bowls. Serve immediately.

SUBSTITUTION TIP: If you can't find radish sprouts, you can substitute watercress or arugula.

SHOYU RAMEN WITH KOREAN-INSPIRED MEATBALLS

30 MINUTES OR LESS, DAIRY-FREE, NUT-FREE
PREP TIME: 15 MINUTES / **COOK TIME:** 15 MINUTES
SERVES 4

Gochujang (Korean fermented red pepper paste) is one of my favorite ingredients, especially as a seasoning for beef. It is spicy, salty, and loaded with umami. It gives these meatballs a ton of flavor and also adds a bit of punch to the glaze on top. You can find gochujang in Korean markets or order it online.

FOR THE MEATBALLS

1 pound ground beef
⅓ cup panko
   bread crumbs
1 large egg, lightly beaten
2 scallions, both white
   and green parts,
   thinly sliced
1½ tablespoons gochujang
2 garlic cloves, minced
2 teaspoons peeled,
   minced fresh ginger
2 teaspoons soy sauce
¼ teaspoon kosher salt
2 tablespoons cooking oil

FOR THE SAUCE

2 tablespoons
   brown sugar
2 teaspoons rice vinegar
2 teaspoons soy sauce
2 teaspoons gochujang

FOR THE SOUP

8 cups Basic Beef
   Broth (page 11) **or**
   store-bought broth
½ cup Basic Shoyu Tare
   (page 18)
18 ounces fresh ramen
   noodles, 12 ounces
   dried ramen noodles,
   or 2 packages instant
   ramen noodles,
   cooked according to
   package directions
4 scallions, both white
   and green parts,
   thinly sliced
2 tablespoons toasted
   sesame seeds

TO MAKE THE MEATBALLS

1. Preheat the oven to 350°F and line a large baking sheet with aluminum foil or parchment paper.

CONTINUED

2. In a medium bowl, combine the ground beef, panko, egg, scallions, gochujang, garlic, ginger, soy sauce, and salt, and mix to combine.

3. Form the mixture into 1½-inch meatballs, making about 16 total. Arrange the meatballs on the prepared baking sheet. Brush the meatballs with the oil.

4. Bake for about 15 minutes, until the meatballs are browned on top and cooked through.

TO MAKE THE SAUCE

5. While the meatballs are cooking, in a small saucepan, stir together the brown sugar, vinegar, soy sauce, and gochujang over medium heat, and bring the mixture to a simmer. Cook, stirring occasionally, for about 5 minutes, until the sauce thickens.

TO MAKE THE SOUP

6. In a pot, heat the broth over medium-high heat until simmering.

7. Into each of 4 serving bowls, put 2 tablespoons of tare. Divide the noodles among the bowls and ladle the broth over the noodles. Top each bowl with a few meatballs. Drizzle the sauce over the meatballs. Garnish with the scallions and sesame seeds and serve immediately.

MAKE AHEAD TIP: You can make the meatballs in advance. Refrigerate them in a covered container for up to 3 days or in the freezer for up to 3 months. To serve, reheat the meatballs in the microwave before adding them to the soup. Frozen meatballs do not need to be thawed before heating.

SHOYU RAMEN WITH BRAISED BEEF BRISKET, SWEET POTATOES, AND DAIKON

DAIRY-FREE, NUT-FREE

PREP TIME: 15 MINUTES / **COOK TIME:** 1 HOUR 55 MINUTES

SERVES 4

Tender braised brisket topping a bowl of shoyu ramen makes for a hearty meal. Flavored with ginger, sake, and soy sauce, this meat stew is delicious on its own when served over rice. Add it to a bowl of ramen, and it is heaven.

FOR THE BEEF AND VEGETABLES

1 tablespoon oil

3 thin slices peeled fresh ginger

1 pound beef brisket, cut into 1½-inch chunks

2½ cups water, divided

½ cup sake

1 tablespoon soy sauce

½ teaspoon sugar

1 medium sweet potato, peeled and cut into 1½-inch chunks

1 daikon radish, cut into 1½-inch chunks

FOR THE SOUP

8 cups Basic Beef Broth (page 11) or store-bought broth

½ cup Basic Shoyu Tare (page 18)

18 ounces fresh ramen noodles, 12 ounces dried ramen noodles, or 2 packages instant ramen noodles, cooked according to package directions

4 scallions, both white and green parts, thinly sliced

TO MAKE THE BEEF AND VEGETABLES

1. In a large saucepan, heat the oil over medium-high heat. Add the ginger and cook, stirring, for about 30 seconds. Add the beef and cook for about 7 minutes, stirring occasionally, until the meat is browned all over.

2. Add 1½ cups of water, the sake, soy sauce, and sugar, and bring to a boil. Reduce the heat to low and simmer for about 1 hour and 15 minutes, stirring occasionally, until the meat is tender.

3. Add the sweet potato, daikon, and the remaining 1 cup of water to the stew. Continue to simmer for about 30 more minutes, until the vegetables are tender.

CONTINUED

TO MAKE THE SOUP

4. In a pot, heat the broth over medium-high heat until simmering.

5. Into each of 4 serving bowls, put 2 tablespoons of tare. Divide the noodles among the bowls and ladle the broth over the noodles. Top each bowl with a few chunks of meat, some of the sweet potato, and some of the daikon. Garnish with the scallions and serve immediately.

MAKE AHEAD TIP: The brisket and vegetables can be cooked in advance and will taste even better after being refrigerated overnight. Store the brisket and vegetables in the refrigerator for up to 3 days or in the freezer for up to 3 months.

*Mushroom Broth
Ramen with Soy Sauce
Eggs and Baby Bok Choy,*
page 132

CHAPTER EIGHT

VEGAN AND VEGETARIAN RAMEN

While most ramen is based on meaty broths and topped with meaty toppings, there are several fun and delicious ways to make really flavorful vegan and vegetarian broth, and the topping options are endless. Even though these ramen bowls are meatless, they can still provide plenty of protein by using higher-protein toppings such as eggs, beans, nuts, seeds, tofu, or tempeh.

For a super-satisfying bowl of vegan or vegetarian ramen, start with a mushroom- or seaweed-based broth and add a rainbow of veggies and other meatless toppings.

MISO RAMEN WITH ROASTED SHIITAKE MUSHROOMS AND GREENS

DAIRY-FREE, GLUTEN-FREE (USE GLUTEN-FREE NOODLES), VEGAN

PREP TIME: 15 MINUTES / **COOK TIME:** 40 MINUTES

SERVES 4

This vegan ramen starts with a simple shiitake mushroom broth. The Basic Miso Tare (page 19) gives it flavor and depth, but if you want a bit of heat, this is also great with Spicy Miso Tare. The crisp-edged roasted mushrooms add a satisfying meatiness, but of course without any meat.

FOR THE MUSHROOMS

1 pound shiitake mushrooms, stemmed

2 tablespoons cooking oil

Kosher salt

Freshly ground black pepper

FOR THE SOUP

8 cups Mushroom Broth (page 14)

½ cup Basic Miso Tare (page 19)

18 ounces fresh ramen noodles, 12 ounces dried ramen noodles, or 2 packages instant ramen noodles, cooked according to package directions

2 cups baby greens

4 scallions, both white and green parts, thinly sliced

TO MAKE THE MUSHROOMS

1. Preheat the oven to 400°F.

2. In a bowl, toss the mushrooms with the oil until they are well coated. Arrange the mushrooms on a large baking sheet in a single layer. Season them with salt and pepper.

3. Roast for 25 minutes, flip the mushrooms over, and roast for about 15 minutes more, until the mushrooms are crisp around the edges.

TO MAKE THE SOUP

4. In a stockpot, heat the broth over medium-high heat, until simmering.

5. Into each of 4 serving bowls, put 2 tablespoons of tare. Divide the noodles among the bowls and ladle the broth over the noodles. Arrange the mushrooms, greens, and scallions on top of the bowls. Serve immediately.

MAKE AHEAD TIP: Make a double or triple batch of mushrooms and store them in the refrigerator for up to 1 week. They're great for snacking, for adding to sandwiches, or for topping more bowls of ramen.

SPICY MISO RAMEN WITH GRILLED TOFU

DAIRY-FREE, VEGAN

PREP TIME: 15 MINUTES, PLUS 1 HOUR TO PRESS AND MARINATE /
COOK TIME: 25 MINUTES

SERVES 4

Marinated and grilled tofu is a flavorful and filling topping for a bowl of vegan ramen. Grilled sweet corn and savory and nutty marinated bean sprouts add texture and flavor. Add a sprinkle of the Japanese spice mixture Shichimi Togarashi (page 31) for an extra kick.

FOR THE TOFU AND CORN

1 (14-ounce) package extra-firm tofu, drained
¼ cup rice vinegar
¼ cup soy sauce
2½ tablespoons cooking oil
1 garlic clove, minced
¼ teaspoon kosher salt
¼ teaspoon freshly ground black pepper
2 ears fresh corn

FOR THE SOUP

8 cups Mushroom Broth (page 14)
½ cup Spicy Miso Tare (page 19)
18 ounces fresh ramen noodles, 12 ounces dried ramen noodles, or 2 packages instant ramen noodles, cooked according to package directions

4 scallions, both white and green parts, thinly sliced
1 cup Marinated Bean Sprouts (page 23) or fresh bean sprouts

TO MAKE THE TOFU AND CORN

1. Wrap the block of tofu in a clean dish towel. Set it on a dinner plate, top it with a second dinner plate, and then put something heavy like a large can of beans or tomatoes on top to press it down. Let the tofu stand for about 30 minutes.

2. Slice the tofu into 5 or 6 slabs.

3. In a baking dish, combine the vinegar, soy sauce, oil, garlic, salt, and pepper, and stir to mix. Add the tofu slices and turn to coat. Cover the dish and refrigerate it for 30 minutes.

4. Heat a grill or grill pan to high heat.

5. Remove the tofu from the marinade and place it on the grill along with the corn.

6. Cook the tofu slabs for 6 to 8 minutes, until the bottom sides have prominent grill marks. Flip them over and cook on the second side for another 6 to 8 minutes, until the grill marks are prominent.

7. Cook the corn, turning occasionally, until it is lightly browned on all sides, about 6 minutes total.

8. Remove the tofu and corn from the grill. Slice the tofu into strips. Using a sharp knife, slice the corn kernels off the ears of corn.

TO MAKE THE SOUP

9. In a stockpot, heat the broth over medium-high heat until simmering.

10. Into each of 4 serving bowls, place 2 tablespoons of tare. Divide the noodles among the bowls and ladle the broth over the noodles. Arrange several strips of tofu, some corn, some scallions, and some sprouts on top of each bowl. Serve immediately.

COOKING TIP: Pressing the excess water out of the tofu gives it a heartier texture and also allows it to soak up more of the flavors from the marinade. Alternatively, you can freeze the tofu overnight and then simmer it in hot water for about 10 minutes before slicing. Press as much water out of the thawed tofu as you can before adding it to the marinade.

SOY MILK RAMEN WITH SOFT-BOILED EGG AND KIMCHI

DAIRY-FREE, VEGETARIAN

PREP TIME: 15 MINUTES / **COOK TIME:** 1 HOUR

SERVES 4

Soy milk ramen originated in the city of Kyoto. This rich and creamy version combines soy milk and shiitake dashi for a sumptuous broth. The popular ramen topping menma, or seasoned bamboo shoots, adds a bit of texture and sweet-salty flavor. Kimchi brings acid, heat, and crunch.

5 cups Mushroom Broth (page 14)

5 cups soy milk

½ cup Basic Miso Tare (page 19)

18 ounces fresh ramen noodles, 12 ounces dried ramen noodles, or 2 packages instant ramen noodles, cooked according to package directions

1 cup kimchi

4 scallions, both white and green parts, thinly sliced

1 cup Seasoned Bamboo Shoots (page 22) **or sliced canned bamboo shoots**

2 Soft-Boiled Eggs (page 27)**, halved**

1. In a stockpot over high heat, combine the broth and soy milk and bring the mixture to a boil. Reduce the heat to medium and simmer for about 60 minutes, uncovered, until the broth reduces by about one-third.

2. Into each of 4 serving bowls, put 2 tablespoons of tare. Divide the noodles among the bowls and ladle the broth over the noodles. Divide the kimchi, scallions, bamboo shoots, and eggs among the bowls and arrange them on top. Serve immediately.

SUBSTITUTION TIP: If you don't have bamboo shoots, substitute Marinated Bean Sprouts (page 23) or fresh bean sprouts.

SPICY MISO AND MUSHROOM RAMEN

30 MINUTES OR LESS, DAIRY-FREE, VEGETARIAN

PREP TIME: 10 MINUTES / **COOK TIME:** 20 MINUTES

SERVES 4

This vegetarian ramen is loaded with umami thanks to the combination of mushroom broth, reconstituted dried shiitake mushrooms, and savory roasted tomatoes. Leave out the eggs to make this a vegan bowl.

8 cups Mushroom Broth
(page 14)

2 ounces dried shiitake mushrooms

½ cup Spicy Miso Tare
(page 19)

18 ounces fresh ramen noodles, 12 ounces dried ramen noodles, or 2 packages instant ramen noodles, cooked according to package directions

12 Roasted Tomato
(page 24) **halves**

2 Soy Sauce Eggs
(page 28), **halved**

4 scallions, both white and green parts, thinly sliced

1. In a stockpot over medium-high heat, combine the broth and mushrooms and bring to a simmer. Simmer for about 20 minutes, until the mushrooms are tender. Remove the mushrooms from the broth, cut them into slices, and reserve them for topping the ramen.

2. Into each of 4 serving bowls, put 2 tablespoons of tare. Divide the noodles among the bowls and ladle the broth over the noodles. Arrange several tomato halves, several mushrooms, and half an egg on top of each bowl. Top with the scallions. Serve immediately.

SUBSTITUTION TIP: If you don't have roasted tomatoes, substitute a pile of assorted mushrooms, cut into slices and sautéed in olive oil with lots of garlic.

KOMBU BROTH RAMEN WITH SWEET POTATOES, CRISPY KALE, AND BAKED TOFU

DAIRY-FREE, NUT-FREE, VEGAN

PREP TIME: 10 MINUTES / **COOK TIME:** 25 MINUTES

SERVES 4

This vegan ramen uses a combination of kombu seaweed broth and shiitake mushroom broth, giving it a deep umami flavor. Crispy kale, tender roasted sweet potatoes, and baked tofu offer texture and flavor, making this a hearty bowl.

FOR THE SWEET POTATOES AND KALE

1 pound sweet potatoes, peeled and diced

2 tablespoons cooking oil, divided

12 kale leaves, tough center stems removed

Kosher salt

Freshly ground black pepper

FOR THE SOUP

4 cups Basic Vegan Broth (page 13)

4 cups Mushroom Broth (page 14)

½ cup Basic Shoyu Tare (page 18)

18 ounces fresh ramen noodles, 12 ounces dried ramen noodles, or 2 packages instant ramen noodles, cooked according to the package directions

1 (8-ounce) package baked tofu, cut into 1-by-3-inch strips

TO MAKE THE SWEET POTATOES AND KALE

1. Preheat the oven to 425°F.

2. On a baking sheet, toss the sweet potatoes with 1 tablespoon of oil and arrange them in a single layer on half of the sheet.

3. On the other half of the baking sheet, toss the kale with the remaining 1 tablespoon of oil, and arrange it on that half of the baking sheet in a single layer.

4. Season both the kale and sweet potatoes with salt and pepper and place them in the oven to roast.

5. After 15 minutes, remove the pan from the oven. Remove the kale from the pan and toss the potatoes around. Return the potatoes to the oven to cook for another 5 to 10 minutes, until they are tender and golden brown.

TO MAKE THE SOUP

6. While the potatoes are cooking, in a stockpot combine the vegan and mushroom broths over medium-high heat and bring them to a simmer.

7. Into each of 4 serving bowls, put 2 tablespoons of tare. Divide the noodles among the bowls and ladle the broth over the noodles. Arrange the tofu strips on top of each bowl along with the sweet potatoes and crispy kale. Serve immediately.

SUBSTITUTION TIP: If you don't have one or the other type of broth (kombu or shiitake), you can use 8 cups of one type.

MUSHROOM BROTH RAMEN WITH SOY SAUCE EGGS AND BABY BOK CHOY

30 MINUTES OR LESS, DAIRY-FREE, NUT-FREE, VEGETARIAN

PREP TIME: 10 MINUTES / **COOK TIME:** 5 MINUTES

SERVES 4

This is a super-simple vegetarian ramen that comes together in minutes as long as you have mushroom broth and soy sauce eggs on hand. If you don't have the eggs ready, you can always substitute plain Soft-Boiled Eggs (page 27), cooked just before putting the soup together.

8 cups Mushroom Broth (page 14)

12 baby bok choy

½ cup Basic Shio Tare (page 17)

18 ounces fresh ramen noodles, 12 ounces dried ramen noodles, or 2 packages instant ramen noodles, cooked according to the package directions

4 Soy Sauce Eggs (page 28), halved

4 scallions, both white and green parts, thinly sliced

1. In a pot, heat the broth over medium-high heat until simmering. Add the bok choy and cook for 3 to 4 minutes, until wilted.

2. Into each of 4 serving bowls, put 2 tablespoons of tare. Divide the noodles among the bowls and ladle the broth over the noodles. Divide the baby bok choy among the bowls and top each bowl with 2 egg halves. Garnish with the scallions. Serve immediately.

MAKE AHEAD TIP: All the elements of this soup can be made ahead. The Soy Sauce Eggs will keep in the refrigerator for up to 3 days. The broth can be kept in the refrigerator for up to 1 week or in the freezer for up to 3 months.

SHOYU RAMEN WITH ROASTED GARLIC, FAVA BEANS, AND ARUGULA

DAIRY-FREE, NUT-FREE, VEGAN

PREP TIME: 10 MINUTES / **COOK TIME:** 50 MINUTES

SERVES 4

Sweet, caramelized roasted garlic adds depth and umami to this vegan bowl. Fava beans give it heft and protein. Radishes and arugula top it off with fresh-from-the-garden flavor.

FOR THE GARLIC AND BEANS

1 garlic head, top sliced off to reveal the cloves

2 tablespoons extra-virgin olive oil, divided

1 pound frozen fava beans, thawed

½ teaspoon kosher salt

FOR THE SOUP

8 cups Basic Vegan Broth (page 13)

½ cup Basic Shoyu Tare (page 18)

18 ounces fresh ramen noodles, 12 ounces dried ramen noodles, or 2 packages instant ramen noodles, cooked according to package directions

4 large radishes, thinly sliced

1 cup arugula

TO MAKE THE GARLIC AND BEANS

1. Preheat the oven to 400°F.

2. Place the head of garlic on a piece of aluminum foil, drizzle 1 tablespoon of oil over the top, and wrap the aluminum foil around the bulb.

3. Roast for about 45 minutes, until the garlic cloves are very soft and browned on top. Squeeze the cloves out of the skin and mash them slightly.

4. In a medium skillet, heat the remaining 1 tablespoon of oil over medium-high heat. Add the beans and salt and cook, stirring, for about 5 minutes, until the beans are heated through and begin to brown.

CONTINUED

SHOYU RAMEN WITH ROASTED GARLIC, FAVA BEANS, AND ARUGULA CONTINUED

TO MAKE THE SOUP

5. In a stockpot, heat the broth over medium-high heat until simmering.

6. Into each of 4 serving bowls, put 2 tablespoons of tare. Divide the noodles among the bowls and ladle the broth over the noodles. Top each bowl with 1 or 2 cloves of the roasted garlic and arrange the beans, radish slices, and arugula on top of the bowls. Serve immediately.

SUBSTITUTION TIP: If you have access to fresh fava beans, you can certainly use them. They are a bit labor intensive, though, since they need to be double peeled. I prefer to use the frozen ones because they are simpler and quicker to prepare.

SHIITAKE MUSHROOM RAMEN WITH SMOKED TOFU, CORN, AND SPINACH

30 MINUTES, DAIRY-FREE, NUT-FREE, VEGAN
PREP TIME: 10 MINUTES / **COOK TIME:** 5 MINUTES
SERVES 4

Another super-quick vegan ramen bowl—this features sweet corn for a fresh flavor and smoked tofu, which adds depth and provides protein. The freshness of the baby spinach helps balance the smoky flavors.

FOR THE CORN
1 teaspoon sesame oil
1½ cups fresh or frozen corn kernels
Pinch salt

FOR THE SOUP
8 cups Mushroom Broth (page 14)
½ cup Basic Shoyu Tare (page 18)

18 ounces fresh ramen noodles, 12 ounces dried ramen noodles, or 2 packages instant ramen noodles, cooked according to package directions
1 (8-ounce) package smoked tofu, cut into strips
2 cups baby spinach

TO MAKE THE CORN

1. In a medium skillet, heat the sesame oil over medium-high heat. Add the corn and salt and cook, stirring, for about 3 minutes, until heated through and just beginning to brown and soften.

TO MAKE THE SOUP

2. In a stockpot, heat the broth over medium-high heat until simmering.

3. Into each of 4 serving bowls, put 2 tablespoons of tare. Divide the noodles among the bowls and ladle the broth over the noodles. Top each bowl with a few strips of tofu, some corn, and some spinach. Serve immediately.

VARIATION TIP: If you have Roasted Tomatoes (page 24) on hand, they would be a great addition to this ramen.

KOMBU RAMEN WITH MARINATED AND SEARED TEMPEH

DAIRY-FREE, VEGAN
PREP TIME: 10 MINUTES, PLUS 30 MINUTES TO MARINATE / **COOK TIME:** 10 MINUTES
SERVES 4

Tempeh, which is made from fermented soybeans, originated in Indonesia. This spicy, peanutty marinade salutes that heritage and makes a delicious, savory, vegan ramen topping that's loaded with protein. You can buy tempeh in most supermarkets, alongside the tofu, or in Asian markets.

FOR THE TEMPEH
2 tablespoons soy sauce
2 tablespoons creamy, no-sugar-added peanut butter
2 tablespoons rice vinegar
2 tablespoons sugar
1 teaspoon chili paste (like sambal oelek)
1 (8-ounce) package tempeh, cut into triangles
1 tablespoon sesame oil

FOR THE SOUP
8 cups Basic Vegan Broth (page 13)
½ cup Basic Shoyu Tare (page 18)
18 ounces fresh ramen noodles, 12 ounces dried ramen noodles, or 2 packages instant ramen noodles, cooked according to package directions

4 scallions, both white and green parts, thinly sliced

TO MAKE THE TEMPEH

1. In a bowl, combine the soy sauce, peanut butter, vinegar, sugar, and chili paste, and stir to mix. Add the tempeh and toss to coat it. Let the tempeh stand for about 30 minutes to marinate.

2. In a large skillet, heat the sesame oil over medium-high heat. Add the tempeh, reserving the marinade, and cook for 4 to 5 minutes per side, until crispy.

TO MAKE THE SOUP

3. In a stockpot, heat the vegan broth over medium-high heat until simmering.

4. Into each of 4 serving bowls, put 2 tablespoons of tare. Divide the noodles among the bowls and ladle the broth over the noodles. Divide the tempeh and scallions among the bowls and drizzle the marinade over the top. Serve immediately.

SUBSTITUTION TIP: If you don't have tempeh, substitute 1 (14-ounce) package of extra-firm tofu. Press out as much water as you can by pressing it under a heavy weight for 30 minutes or so before slicing and marinating.

Shrimp and Vegetable Ramen Salad with Yuzu Vinaigrette, **page 154**

CHAPTER NINE

RAMEN REMIXED

The tradition of ramen may have started in Japan, but it was based on older Chinese-style noodle dishes. As its popularity has spread across the globe, ramen has continued to evolve. Unlike many other aspects of Japanese cuisine, ramen is not bound by tradition but rather is a constantly evolving dish built on innovation and creative interpretation. While we think of "traditional" ramen as being broth + tare + noodles + toppings, ramen can be served in many other exciting ways. The best ramen chefs create their recipes based on the meat, fish, and produce available in their local markets and add their own flair.

The ramen dishes in this chapter stray far from the original equation of traditional ramen. They are fun, adventurous takes on ramen noodles, both with and without broth. They use non-Japanese ingredients, such as tomatoes, pineapple, and cheese, and different cooking and serving methods, including stir-fried and chilled.

TANTANMEN WITH SPICY SESAME PORK

**30 MINUTES OR LESS, DAIRY-FREE, GLUTEN-FREE (USE GLUTEN-FREE NOODLES),
NUT-FREE OPTION**
PREP TIME: 10 MINUTES / **COOK TIME:** 10 MINUTES
SERVES 4

Dan dan noodles is a Chinese noodle dish in which lo mein noodles
are topped with ground pork and a spicy sauce of sesame paste,
Szechuan peppercorns, hot chili oil, and rice wine. Tantanmen is a
Japanese version of dan dan noodles, using ramen noodles and
pork broth.

FOR THE PORK
1 pound ground pork
2 garlic cloves, minced
2 tablespoons peeled,
   minced fresh ginger
4 scallions, both white
   and green parts, thinly
   sliced and separated
2 tablespoons
   doubanjiang
   (fermented
   chile-bean paste)
1 tablespoon
   Japanese or Chinese
   sesame paste
½ teaspoon
   Szechuan peppercorns

FOR THE SOUP
8 cups Basic Pork
   Broth (page 10) **or**
   store-bought broth
½ cup Spicy Miso Tare
   (page 19)

18 ounces fresh ramen
   noodles, 12 ounces
   dried ramen noodles,
   or 2 packages instant
   ramen noodles,
   cooked according to
   package directions
4 teaspoons
   Sesame-Chili
   Oil (page 30) **or**
   store-bought chili oil

TO MAKE THE PORK

1. In a large skillet, cook the pork over medium-high heat for about
    5 minutes, stirring frequently, until the meat is browned. Add the garlic,
    ginger, and white parts of the scallions, and cook for 1 minute more. Stir in
    the doubanjiang, sesame paste, and Szechuan peppercorns, and cook for
    1 minute more. Remove the skillet from the heat.

TO MAKE THE SOUP

2. In a pot, heat the broth over medium-high heat until simmering.

3. Into each of 4 serving bowls, put 2 tablespoons of tare. Divide the noodles among the bowls and ladle the broth over the noodles. Top each bowl with the pork, scallion greens, and chili oil. Serve immediately.

VARIATION TIP: Make this tantanmen "Hiroshima style" without broth. Add 1 tablespoon of sake, 1 tablespoon of white miso paste, and 1 cup of water to the pork at the end of step 1 and simmer for about 5 minutes. Divide the noodles between 4 bowls, top with the pork and sauce mixture, and garnish with the scallion greens and chili oil.

LAKSA-STYLE RAMEN WITH SOFT-BOILED EGGS, GREEN BEANS, AND BEAN SPROUTS

30 MINUTES OR LESS, DAIRY-FREE, GLUTEN-FREE (USE GLUTEN-FREE NOODLES)
PREP TIME: 10 MINUTES / **COOK TIME:** 15 MINUTES
SERVES 4

Laksa is a spicy soup made with coconut milk and the intense flavors of Malaysian cuisine. This brothy noodle soup is flavored with laksa paste, which is similar to curry paste. Different regions and cooks have their own distinctive styles of laksa paste, usually containing chiles, lemongrass, cumin, turmeric, ginger or galangal, and other seasonings. You can buy laksa paste in Asian markets. This store-bought seasoning paste makes it easy to whip up a bowl of the soup. And turning it into a ramen is a no-brainer if you love ramen and spicy food.

FOR THE LAKSA BROTH

1 tablespoon cooking oil
2 tablespoons peeled, minced fresh ginger
3 garlic cloves, minced
1 cup laksa paste
1 lemongrass stalk, very thinly sliced
6 cups Basic Chicken Broth (page 9) or water
2 (13.5-ounce) cans coconut milk
8 ounces green beans, cut into 2-inch pieces
1 tablespoon fish sauce
Juice of 1 lime

FOR THE SOUP

18 ounces fresh ramen noodles, 12 ounces dried ramen noodles, or 2 packages instant ramen noodles, cooked according to package directions

4 Soft-Boiled Eggs (page 27), halved
1 cup bean sprouts
¼ cup chopped fresh cilantro

TO MAKE THE LAKSA BROTH

1. In a medium saucepan, heat the oil over medium heat. Add the ginger and garlic and cook, stirring, for about 30 seconds. Add the laksa paste and lemongrass and cook, stirring, for 2 to 3 minutes.

2. Add the broth and coconut milk and bring the mixture to a simmer. Cover and let simmer for about 5 minutes.

3. Add the green beans and fish sauce, cover again, and simmer for about 5 minutes more, until the green beans are tender.

4. Just before serving, stir in the lime juice.

TO MAKE THE SOUP

5. Divide the noodles evenly between 4 serving bowls. Ladle the laksa broth and green beans over the noodles. Top each bowl with 2 egg halves and some bean sprouts. Garnish with the cilantro and serve immediately.

SUBSTITUTION TIP: f you can't find laksa paste, substitute Thai red curry paste, but use less. Start with ¼ cup and add more as needed to achieve your desired spice level.

YAKISOBA-STYLE RAMEN WITH GARLIC, CHILI, AND SESAME OIL

30 MINUTES OR LESS, DAIRY-FREE, NUT-FREE, VEGAN
PREP TIME: 10 MINUTES / **COOK TIME:** 10 MINUTES
SERVES 4

This yakisoba-style ramen is a quick stir-fried noodle dish that is a popular street food in Japan. You'll often see it cooked with pork, shrimp, or tofu and garnished with shredded cabbage, bean sprouts, and shredded carrots. This vegan version has lots of garlic and a kick of spice from chili paste.

2 tablespoons cooking oil
1 (14-ounce) package firm tofu, pressed and cut into chunks
2 garlic cloves, minced
⅓ cup soy sauce
2 teaspoons brown sugar
1 to 2 tablespoons chili paste

18 ounces fresh ramen noodles, 12 ounces dried noodles, or 2 packages instant ramen noodles, cooked al dente (1 minute less than the package directions for fresh ramen, 2 minutes less for dried ramen, and 30 seconds less for instant ramen)

2 scallions, both white and green parts, thinly sliced
1 tablespoon toasted sesame seeds
2 teaspoons sesame oil

1. In a large skillet, heat the oil over medium heat. Add the tofu and cook for about 5 minutes, stirring occasionally, until the tofu begins to brown. Add the garlic and cook, stirring, for 20 seconds more, until fragrant.

2. Stir in the soy sauce, brown sugar, and chili paste, and then immediately add the noodles. Toss the noodles in the sauce until they are well coated and remove the skillet from the heat.

3. Serve hot, garnished with the scallions, sesame seeds, and sesame oil.

SUBSTITUTION TIP: Substitute thinly sliced pork or peeled and deveined shrimp for the tofu.

THAI GREEN CURRY RAMEN WITH CHICKEN

30 MINUTES OR LESS, DAIRY-FREE

PREP TIME: 10 MINUTES / **COOK TIME:** 15 MINUTES

SERVES 4

Spicy Thai green curry paste, creamy coconut milk, and chicken broth make an addictive medium for tender ramen noodles. Red bell peppers add sweetness, crunch, and color. Don't forget the squeeze of lime as it gives just the right burst of acid to bring it all together.

2 tablespoons cooking oil

1 to 3 tablespoons Thai green curry paste

1 tablespoon peeled, minced fresh ginger

1 garlic clove, minced

1 tablespoon brown sugar

6⅓ cups Basic Chicken Broth (page 9) or store-bought broth

1 (13.5-ounce) can coconut milk

1 tablespoon fish sauce

18 ounces fresh ramen noodles, 12 ounces dried ramen noodles, or 2 packages instant ramen noodles, cooked according to package directions

2 cooked skinless, boneless chicken breasts, sliced

1 red bell pepper, thinly sliced

¼ cup chopped fresh cilantro

1 lime, cut into wedges

1. In a stockpot, heat the oil over medium heat. Add the curry paste, ginger, and garlic, and cook, stirring, for 1 to 2 minutes, until fragrant. Add the sugar and cook, stirring, for 1 minute more.

2. Add the broth, coconut milk, and fish sauce, and bring to a simmer. Reduce the heat if needed to prevent boiling, and simmer for 10 minutes.

3. Divide the noodles between 4 serving bowls. Ladle the broth over the noodles and top each bowl with several slices of chicken, some bell pepper slices, some cilantro, and a wedge of lime. Serve immediately.

SUBSTITUTION TIP: I love using simple poached or steamed chicken breast here, but you can also use rotisserie chicken or grilled chicken. You could also use grilled steak or make it vegetarian with grilled or baked tofu and vegan broth (but check to make sure your curry paste is vegetarian and substitute soy sauce for the fish sauce).

PINEAPPLE RAMEN WITH HAM, NORI STRIPS, AND CORN

30 MINUTES OR LESS, DAIRY-FREE, GLUTEN-FREE (USE GLUTEN-FREE NOODLES), NUT-FREE

PREP TIME: 10 MINUTES / **COOK TIME:** 5 MINUTES

SERVES 4

There is a ramen shop in Tokyo that specializes in savory dishes centered around pineapple. It has a giant ring of pineapple for a sign, and you get an unmistakable (and delicious) whiff of the tropical fruit as you approach. Pineapple may seem like an unlikely ramen ingredient, but it works surprisingly well with the savory flavors of pork broth and ham.

7 cups Basic Pork Broth (page 10) **or store-bought broth**

1 cup pineapple juice

½ cup Basic Shio Tare (page 17)

18 ounces fresh ramen noodles, 12 ounces dried ramen noodles, or 2 packages instant ramen noodles, cooked according to package

8 ounces cooked ham, diced

1 cup diced fresh pineapple

1 cup fresh or frozen (thawed) corn kernels

1 cup bean sprouts

1 sheet nori, cut into strips

1. In a stockpot, heat the broth until simmering. Add the pineapple juice and bring the pot back to a simmer.

2. Into each of 4 serving bowls, put 2 tablespoons of tare. Divide the noodles among the bowls and ladle the broth over the noodles. Arrange the ham, pineapple, corn, and bean sprouts on top of the bowls and garnish with the nori. Serve immediately.

VARIATION TIP: Garnish the soup with fresh herbs. Either cilantro or basil would pair beautifully with the pineapple.

CHEESY SHOYU RAMEN

30 MINUTES OR LESS, NUT-FREE, ONE-POT
PREP TIME: 5 MINUTES / **COOK TIME:** 5 MINUTES
SERVES 4

At first glance, the whole idea of cheese ramen sounds like a late-night concoction cooked up by inebriated college students. In reality, it was popularized by none other than celebrity chef Roy Choi. I love cheese and I love ramen, so this combo was an easy yes for me. You can use any cheese, from a pungent, hard-grating cheese like Parmesan to a creamy brie. I've embraced the "dorm food" approach here with sliced American cheese. In keeping with that genre, this is one of the easiest bowls of ramen you can make.

8 cups Basic Chicken Broth (page 9) **or store-bought broth**
½ cup Basic Shoyu Tare (page 18)

18 ounces fresh ramen noodles, 12 ounces dried ramen noodles, or 2 packages instant ramen noodles, cooked according to package directions
4 slices American cheese

4 Soft-Boiled Eggs (page 27)**, halved**
4 scallions, both white and green parts, thinly sliced
2 teaspoons Shichimi Togarashi (page 31)

1. In a stockpot, heat the broth over medium-high heat until simmering.

2. Into each of 4 serving bowls, place 2 tablespoons of the tare. Divide the noodles among the bowls and ladle the broth over the noodles. Top each bowl with 1 slice of cheese and 2 egg halves. Sprinkle the scallions and shichimi togarashi over the top and serve immediately.

SUBSTITUTION TIP: If you don't have shichimi togarashi, substitute 4 teaspoons Sesame-Chili Oil (page 30) or store-bought chili oil.

TOMATO RAMEN WITH CHEESE AND NORI STRIPS

30 MINUTES OR LESS, GLUTEN-FREE (USE GLUTEN-FREE NOODLES), NUT-FREE OPTION, VEGETARIAN

PREP TIME: 10 MINUTES / **COOK TIME:** 15 MINUTES

SERVES 4

This is another variation on cheese ramen, but this one has a tomato soup base. It reminds me of the tomato soup and grilled cheese sandwich combo I loved so much as a kid. If it's raining outside, just give me a bowl of this soup, and I'm happy.

2 cups water

1 (28-ounce) can crushed tomatoes

1 tablespoon tomato paste

2 tablespoons butter

½ cup Basic Miso Tare (page 19)

18 ounces fresh ramen noodles, 12 ounces dried ramen noodles, or 2 packages instant ramen noodles, cooked according to package directions

1 cup shredded aged Gouda cheese

4 scallions, both white and green parts, thinly sliced

1 nori sheet, cut into 3-by-1-inch strips

1. In a stockpot, combine the water, tomatoes and their juices, and tomato paste, and bring to a boil over high heat. Reduce the heat to medium-low, cover the pot, and simmer for 15 minutes. Add the butter.

2. Using an immersion blender or in a countertop blender (in batches), puree the soup. Return the soup to the pot and reheat it if needed.

3. Into each of 4 serving bowls, put 2 tablespoons of tare. Divide the noodles among the bowls and ladle the soup over the noodles. Divide the cheese, scallions, and nori strips among the bowls. Serve immediately.

SUBSTITUTION TIP: Go ahead and use canned tomato soup for this recipe if you like. I would advise against using one with strong flavors like basil or Italian seasonings. Opt instead for a simple condensed tomato soup made with half water and half milk.

SPICY PEANUT SAUCE RAMEN NOODLES WITH TOFU AND GREEN BEANS

30 MINUTES OR LESS, DAIRY-FREE, VEGAN
PREP TIME: 10 MINUTES / **COOK TIME:** 20 MINUTES
SERVES 4

Peanut sauce is one of my all-time favorite foods, so I had to try putting it on ramen noodles. This is a yakisoba-style ramen, meaning the noodles are stir-fried in a skillet (after they're cooked according to the package directions) and there is no broth.

2 tablespoons cooking oil

1 (14-ounce) package firm tofu, excess water pressed out and cut into cubes

1 cup warm water

½ cup no-sugar-added creamy peanut butter

6 tablespoons Thai sweet chili sauce

2 tablespoons soy sauce

Juice of 1 lime

1 teaspoon chili paste (like sambal oelek)

1½ cups fresh or frozen green beans, cut into 2-inch pieces

18 ounces fresh ramen noodles, 12 ounces dried ramen noodles, or 2 packages instant ramen noodles, cooked according to package directions

4 scallions, both white and green parts, thinly sliced

1. In a large skillet, heat the oil over medium heat. Add the tofu and cook for 8 minutes, stirring occasionally, until the tofu is browned.

2. Meanwhile, in a small bowl, stir together the water, peanut butter, chili sauce, soy sauce, lime juice, and chili paste. Stir to mix.

3. Add the green beans to the skillet and then add the peanut butter mixture. Cook for about 5 minutes, stirring occasionally, until the green beans are tender.

4. Add the noodles to the skillet and toss to coat them in the sauce. Cook, stirring occasionally, for about 5 minutes, until heated through.

5. Serve immediately, garnished with the scallions.

INGREDIENT TIP: Thai sweet chili sauce is the same sweet-spicy sauce you get in Thai restaurants for dipping spring rolls and fish cakes in. You can buy it in many supermarkets or in Asian markets.

SPICY CHICKEN MAZEMEN

30 MINUTES OR LESS, DAIRY-FREE, NUT-FREE
PREP TIME: 10 MINUTES / **COOK TIME:** 10 MINUTES
SERVES 4

Mazemen refers to noodles served with sauce rather than broth. Just before eating, the sauce, toppings, and noodles are mixed together so that the noodles get nicely coated. This one includes spicy ground chicken and chard. Soft-boiled eggs thicken the sauce and help it stick better to the noodles.

1 tablespoon cooking oil

1 pound ground chicken

½ teaspoon kosher salt

1 tablespoon peeled, minced fresh ginger

1 garlic clove, minced

1½ cups Basic Chicken Broth (page 9) or store-bought broth

2 teaspoons chili paste (like sambal oelek)

1 teaspoon soy sauce

8 chard leaves, tough center stems removed and leaves julienned

18 ounces fresh ramen noodles, 12 ounces dried ramen noodles, or 2 packages instant ramen noodles, cooked according to package directions

4 Soft-Boiled Eggs (page 27), halved

4 scallions, both white and green parts, thinly sliced

1. In a large skillet, heat the oil over medium heat. Add the chicken and salt and cook for about 4 minutes, stirring occasionally, until the meat is browned. Add the ginger and garlic and cook for 1 minute more, until fragrant. Add the broth, chili paste, and soy sauce, and stir to combine.

2. When the sauce returns to a simmer, add the chard and cook for about 4 minutes, stirring occasionally, until it is wilted and the sauce thickens.

3. To serve, divide the noodles between 4 serving bowls. Divide the chicken, chard, and eggs between the bowls. Serve immediately, garnished with the scallions.

SUBSTITUTION TIP: You can substitute any ground meat for the chicken—turkey, pork, beef, or even lamb.

COLD VEGAN MAZEMEN WITH CUCUMBERS AND MISO-SESAME SAUCE

30 MINUTES OR LESS, DAIRY-FREE, GLUTEN-FREE (USE GLUTEN-FREE NOODLES), NUT-FREE, VEGAN

PREP TIME: 10 MINUTES

SERVES 4

This cold vegan mazemen is dressed in a thick, flavorful miso-sesame sauce. Lime juice gives it a punch of acid. Cucumbers add a nice bit of crunch. If you like it spicy, add some Sesame-Chili Oil (page 30) or use store-bought chili oil. Feel free to add cubed tofu or tempeh if you want a more protein-heavy dish.

½ cup white miso paste

Juice of 2 limes

4 teaspoons sesame oil

4 teaspoons brown sugar

¼ cup vegetable oil

18 ounces fresh ramen noodles, 12 ounces dried ramen noodles, or 2 packages instant ramen noodles, cooked according to package directions and then rinsed in cold water

2 Japanese or Persian cucumbers, diced

4 scallions, both white and green parts, thinly sliced

2 tablespoons toasted sesame seeds

1. In a large bowl, stir together the miso paste, lime juice, sesame oil, and brown sugar to mix. Whisk in the vegetable oil until the mixture is well combined.

2. Add the noodles to the bowl and toss to coat them with the sauce. Add the cucumbers and scallions and toss again to combine.

3. Serve immediately, garnished with the sesame seeds.

MAKE AHEAD TIP: Since these noodles are served cold, they make a perfect dish to have for leftovers. They'll keep in the refrigerator for up to 3 days. Add the sesame seeds just before serving.

TSUKEMEN WITH GRILLED STEAK

DAIRY-FREE, NUT-FREE

PREP TIME: 10 MINUTES / **COOK TIME:** 30 MINUTES

SERVES 4

Tsukemen is a dish that originated in Tokyo in the early 1960s. Rather than being noodles in broth, it is cold noodles served alongside a thick broth that is used for dipping. This version includes juicy grilled flank steak, savory seasoned bamboo shoots, and rich soft-boiled eggs.

1 pound flank steak

1½ teaspoons sesame oil

1 teaspoon kosher salt

½ teaspoon freshly ground black pepper

2 tablespoons cooking oil

2 garlic cloves, minced

2 tablespoons peeled, minced fresh ginger

8 cups Basic Chicken Broth (page 9) **or** store-bought broth

½ cup **Basic Shoyu Tare** (page 18)

18 ounces fresh ramen noodles, 12 ounces dried ramen noodles, or 2 packages instant ramen noodles, cooked according to package directions and then rinsed in cold water (refrigerated if made ahead)

2 Soft-Boiled Eggs (page 27), halved lengthwise

1 cup Seasoned Bamboo Shoots (page 22)

4 scallions, both white and green parts, thinly sliced

1. Heat a grill or grill pan over medium-high heat.

2. Rub the steak all over with the sesame oil and season it with the salt and pepper.

3. Grill the steak, flipping it one time, until it is cooked to your desired doneness, 6 to 8 minutes for medium-rare.

4. Transfer the steak to a cutting board and let it stand, uncovered, for 5 minutes. Thinly slice the steak across the grain.

5. In a large saucepan, heat the oil over medium-high heat. Add the garlic and ginger and cook for 1 minute, stirring, until fragrant. Add the broth and bring just to a boil. Reduce the heat to medium-low and stir in the tare. Simmer, uncovered, for 20 minutes.

6. To serve, divide the broth among 4 serving bowls. Divide the noodles into 4 separate serving bowls and top each with several slices of the steak and half an egg. Place the bamboo shoots and scallions on top. Serve immediately, giving each person a bowl of noodles and a bowl of broth.

SUBSTITUTION TIP: You can use any type of broth you like here—chicken, pork, beef, shiitake, seaweed, or a combination.

SHRIMP AND VEGETABLE RAMEN SALAD WITH YUZU VINAIGRETTE

30 MINUTES OR LESS, DAIRY-FREE, GLUTEN-FREE (USE GLUTEN-FREE NOODLES), NUT-FREE

PREP TIME: 10 MINUTES

SERVES 4

Ramen salad is just what it sounds like—noodles and vegetables tossed with a tart salad dressing. It's a refreshing way to eat ramen on a warm summer day. Yuzu, used in the dressing, is a tangerine-size citrus grown in Japan. It is used for its juice, which is puckeringly tart, and its fragrant zest. Fresh yuzu can be difficult to find here, but you can buy yuzu juice in bottles at Japanese or Asian markets. If you can't find yuzu juice, substitute lime juice with a splash of orange juice added.

FOR THE VINAIGRETTE
2 tablespoons yuzu juice

1 tablespoon Dijon mustard

Zest of 1 lemon

½ teaspoon kosher salt

¼ teaspoon freshly ground black pepper

¼ cup olive or safflower oil

FOR THE SALAD
18 ounces fresh ramen noodles, 12 ounces dried ramen noodles, or 2 packages instant ramen noodles, cooked according to package directions and then rinsed in cold water (refrigerated if made ahead)

2 small Japanese or Persian cucumbers, diced

12 ounces cooked shrimp

10 grape or cherry tomatoes, halved or quartered if large

1 carrot, peeled and shredded

4 scallions, both white and green parts, thinly sliced

TO MAKE THE VINAIGRETTE

1. In a small bowl, whisk the yuzu juice, mustard, lemon zest, salt, and pepper. Add the oil and whisk again until the mixture emulsifies.

TO MAKE THE SALAD

2. In a large bowl, toss together the noodles, cucumbers, shrimp, tomatoes, carrot, and scallions. Add the dressing and toss to coat. Serve immediately.

MAKE AHEAD TIP: You can cook the noodles and mix the vinaigrette ahead of time. Keep both in the refrigerator for up to 3 days. Toss the noodles, dressing, vegetables, and shrimp together just before serving.

MEASUREMENT CONVERSIONS

VOLUME EQUIVALENTS	U.S. STANDARD	U.S. STANDARD (OUNCES)	METRIC (APPROXIMATE)
LIQUID	2 tablespoons	1 fl. oz.	30 mL
	¼ cup	2 fl. oz.	60 mL
	½ cup	4 fl. oz.	120 mL
	1 cup	8 fl. oz.	240 mL
	1½ cups	12 fl. oz.	355 mL
	2 cups or 1 pint	16 fl. oz.	475 mL
	4 cups or 1 quart	32 fl. oz.	1 L
	1 gallon	128 fl. oz.	4 L
DRY	⅛ teaspoon	–	0.5 mL
	¼ teaspoon	–	1 mL
	½ teaspoon	–	2 mL
	¾ teaspoon	–	4 mL
	1 teaspoon	–	5 mL
	1 tablespoon	–	15 mL
	¼ cup	–	59 mL
	⅓ cup	–	79 mL
	½ cup	–	118 mL
	⅔ cup	–	156 mL
	¾ cup	–	177 mL
	1 cup	–	235 mL
	2 cups or 1 pint	–	475 mL
	3 cups	–	700 mL
	4 cups or 1 quart	–	1 L
	½ gallon	–	2 L
	1 gallon	–	4 L

OVEN TEMPERATURES

FAHRENHEIT	CELSIUS (APPROXIMATE)
250°F	120°C
300°F	150°C
325°F	165°C
350°F	180°C
375°F	190°C
400°F	200°C
425°F	220°C
450°F	230°C

WEIGHT EQUIVALENTS

U.S. STANDARD	METRIC (APPROXIMATE)
½ ounce	15 g
1 ounce	30 g
2 ounces	60 g
4 ounces	115 g
8 ounces	225 g
12 ounces	340 g
16 ounces or 1 pound	455 g

INDEX

ACKNOWLEDGMENTS

As always, I am grateful to my husband and son for their constant support and insatiable appetites for ramen. I also wish to thank Jesse Aylen, Kelly Koester, Angela Navarra, Sara Feinstein, Rachel Taenzler, and Katherine Green for their patience, expertise, and support in creating this cookbook.

ABOUT THE AUTHOR

ROBIN DONOVAN is a cookbook author, recipe developer, and food blogger who is obsessed with Japanese food. She is the author of *Sushi at Home*, coauthor of *Ramen Obsession*, and author of several other bestselling cookbooks, including *Campfire Cuisine: Gourmet Recipes for the Great Outdoors*. From her home base in Berkeley, California, she blogs about easy international recipes for people who love food at **AllWaysDelicious.com**.